Milligan

Dominic Behan has had several books published: *Teems of Times and Happy Returns* (1961), *Ireland Sings* (1962), *My Brother, Brendan* (1965) and *The Singing Irish* (1965). He has written a number of plays for radio and television, including *Carson Country*, *The Folksinger*, and an episode for *Churchill's People*. Other works include his plays: *The Patriot Game* (1967), *Posterity Bedamned* (performed in Dublin and London in the early sixties); and many ballad-operas and musical programmes for the old Third Programme of the BBC.

Dominic Behan has also contributed regularly to several magazines and newspapers: *Life Magazine*, *Hibernia Magazine*, the *Dublin Evening Herald* and the *Scotsman*. He was a radio critic for the Scottish *Sunday Standard* and has hosted 'chat' shows for Tyne-Tees Television (*Abroad with Behan*); Radio Telefis Eireann (*Saturday Live*); and more recently a music programme (*A Better Class of Folk*) for Scottish Television.

He lives in Glasgow; and is currently writing a play for the Wildcat Company of Glasgow. He has known Spike Milligan for over thirty years.

DOMINIC BEHAN

Milligan

The Life and Times of Spike Milligan

Methuen · Mandarin

A Mandarin Paperback

MILLIGAN

First published in Great Britain 1988
by Methuen London
This edition published 1989
by Methuen · Mandarin
Michelin House, 81 Fulham Road, London SW3 6RB

Mandarin is an imprint of the Octopus Publishing Group

Copyright © Dominic Behan 1988

A CIP catalogue record for this book is available
from the British Library

ISBN: 0 7493 0155 4

Printed in Great Britain
by Cox & Wyman Ltd, Reading

To Spike,
with affection and deep regard

Contents

List of Illustrations   ix
Acknowledgements   x
Preface   xi

1 A Grand Year for Mushrooms   1
2 Mercenary Mendicants   9
3 Yes Surrender!   15
4 Daddy's Dressed in Khaki   23
5 The Connaught Rangers   30
6 India! India!   39
7 Finger Painting   48
8 London Pride   55
9 England Home and Beauty   61
10 The Wonderful World of Want   68
11 Love's Young Dream   78
12 The Good Soldier Spike   87
13 A Land Fit for Heroes   94
14 The Minstrel Boy   100
15 The D-day Dodgers   108
16 Goodbye to All That   117
17 On the Road   125
18 Sorcerer's Apprentice?   133
19 The Goon Show   140
20 The Swinging Sixties   149
21 Who Goes with Fergus?   156
22 All for Thespis?   163

Notes   175
Appendix   179
General Bibliography   181
Milligan in Print   183

Milligan on TV and Radio   184
Milligan on Celluloid   185
Milligan on Disc   186
Milligan and Company (on disc)   188
Index   189

List of Illustrations

1a Spike Milligan's parents, 1922
b Spike Milligan with his brother and friends, 1932
2 Spike Milligan, 1958
3a *The Goon Show* trio, 1954
b The Goons together after twelve years, 1972
4a Prince Charles visits the Goons, 1964
b Spike Milligan with Eric Sykes, 1984
5a Spike Milligan helps the Family Planning Association with his art exhibition, 1965
b Spike Milligan takes a petition to 10, Downing Street, 1979
6 Spike Milligan addresses a rally organized by Greenpeace, 1978
7 Spike Milligan in *Treasure Island*, 1974
8 'Milligan 'N' Melly', 1973

Acknowledgements

To Geoffrey Strachan, the most talented of editors, from whom I learnt the nature of icebergs.

To Shelagh Milligan, for her charming forbearance.

To Pauline Scudamore, for being a nice lady and a fine biographer.

Acknowledgements and thanks for permission to reproduce photographs are due to the following for the black and white photographs: Spike Milligan and Pauline Scudamore for plates 1a, 1b and 4a; Spike Milligan and the BBC for plate 2, © BBC; Popperfoto for plates 3a, 3b, 5a, 6 and 7, © Popperfoto; Universal Pictorial Press for plate 4b; Keystone Collection for plate 5b, © Keystone Collection; London Weekend Television for plate 8.

Preface

Milligan is really a jack of all politics, and servant of none. He sees everything in its place as part of an ordained order. He feels that trees and flowers are the lungs of the world and that we are idiots if we clog them up to such an extent that they cannot breathe for us.

Listening in silence to Spike Milligan's mind, brooding in concentration on the death of Lucy Gates, we may well think that few modern writers have done more to save children from abuse.

> *Above her bones*
> *Carve out the one word*
> *Why*

is not a question. It is an indictment. He is accusing the innocent as well as the guilty – refusing to accept ignorance as an excuse for adult dereliction.

In Milligan, ingenuousness and genius seem to go hand in hand. If we lose the Welfare State we will lose our grip on the future: there's a place in society for both Francis of Assisi and Robert Owen. For Milligan, the Reds will never get there without the Greens, and that's as dogmatic as he's likely to get.

That is, apart from his cherished cultural-national, and nationally cultural, dogma – Ireland. I know what Spike means, though to understand what he means I sometimes think that you've got to know Milligan. When Spike is not telling us that his father had, like Yeats, a penchant for cowboy books, he's fond of saying that his father was 'imbued with the lateral thinking of the Irish'. Frequently he'll ask, 'Why the hell are we Irish so clever?' But only super-chauvinists and racists of the Eysenk breed would deny that, given the same disadvantages, any other race might have fared just as well.

A resilient people thrives on adversity; for, if necessity is not the mother of invention, it at least spurs ingenuity. The first conquest of Ireland, which started with Henry II in 1177, only began to bite with the Statutes of Kilkenny in 1366. The Irish language was proscribed and, unless you talked in English, Latin, or French, you said nothing. The very mention of the name 'Ireland' was not allowed – it had national connotations. The result of this proscription was that poets, peasants and playwrights had to resort to coded subterfuge if they wanted to refer to their homeland.

Had there not been the need, would anybody recognize 'Rosin Dubh', 'Kathleen ni Houlihaun', or 'Kathleen Mavourneen' as code names for Ireland? As for the 'plain people' of Ireland forced to write and talk in English, Latin or French, while thinking in Gaelic? Well, that all mankind should be so distressed. I sometimes think that *The Goon Show* and *Finnegans Wake!* originated in the Statutes of Kilkenny.

I have attempted to place Milligan in the context of the Irishness I have described because this is what is so exciting about a man who bathes in public. Most of Spike shows over the top of the waves, but yet there is a great deal unseen and unheard.

Some biographers look at their subject through the eyes of friends, acquaintances and enemies. I couldn't find any of Spike's enemies, and his friends had said all they had to say a long time ago. Anyway, I thought to look at his world, if not through Milligan's eyes, then through his mouth.

I have known Spike Milligan for over thirty years; but most of the facts of his life given in this account come from what he has told me about his family and himself in a series of wide-ranging conversations we had together during this, his seventieth year. If his memory is accurate the picture should be all right in a remembrance of times past, a joy in the present, and hope for the future.

I have tried to avoid repeating what has already been written of the published Spike; and of his adult life I have depended on thumbnail sketches rather than pedantic portraiture, because that, you see, is the way he speaks. There is a lot of 'Topsy' in Milligan. I mention most of his works, and quote from a good deal of them, but I have always believed that a good singer should allow the words of a song to sing for themselves.

His Irishry I have stressed because Milligan is Irish, and he has gone to great lengths to prove it. To know Spike you must know the country of his forbears; to know his forbears you must understand the politics of the places to which he has been. People who learned, time without memory, that the embrace of the invader was as lethal as it was loving have a naturally perverted idea of aesthetics, but then, there is beauty in violence too: otherwise, how did we ever see the two days?

Dominic Behan
Glasgow, 1988.

One A Grand Year for Mushrooms

Spike Milligan was born a private, in India, on 16th April, 1918. His father, Leo, was a corporal in the Royal Artillery; his mother, Flo, the daughter of Trumpet Sergeant A. H. Kettleband of the Indian Army who, said his grandson:

> *lay to attention even in bed.**

'Born on the regimental strength', Spike was christened Terence Alan. He says that the family on both sides had been gunners from the siege of Lucknow. Indeed since that particular bit of the Indian mutiny occurred in 1857, there must have been a Milligan in the British Army for twenty years before that.

His great-grandfather, Michael Milligan, took the shilling from the Royal Artillery in Buncrana, County Donegal, at the age of eighteen. The year was 1835.

It has always, by the Irish, been considered a shameful act for an Irishman to join the ranks of the occupying army. Especially to the inhabitants of Donegal. To that godforsaken wilderness the Milligans had been consigned when the best of Ulster, the green fields, were grabbed by penniless presbyterian predators who had arrived in Antrim hungry for the land of the natives.

But patriotism, when not being the scourge of economics, is the child of need. The decision to enlist had little to do with either politics or principles. Poor people become soldiers or paupers. Spike sees it quite philosophically:

> *His parents thought, 'This boy is not going to live unless we get him to join up.' Most of the lads that fought at Waterloo, you know, were Irish lads from Irish regiments. But for the potato*

*This and all quotes set in italics are Spike Milligan in conversation with the author, unless otherwise attributed.

famines the Duke of Wellington wouldn't have had a bloody army!

Milligan has a mind like blotting paper, though more eclectic. He remembers everything and knows that every man is conditioned by the past. His Catholic Christianity is of the same spring as the Kennedys – need. 'Forgive your enemies, but remember their names.' Since nobody but the oppressed notices serfs or soldiers his art would always be in the best Irish tradition of Joyce, though not for him the symbol of all Irish art: 'The cracked looking-glass of a servant.'

He's not surprised therefore that the questionably altruistic bravery of his countrymen went unrewarded. That very same siege of Lucknow, in which his forbears had been involved, had been relieved because of the action of an Irishman, Henry Kavanagh, who:

> *. . . squirmed through the sepoy lines, swam the Gumti, and made contact with [Sir Colin] Campbell's force some miles beyond the city.*[1]

It's a wise man who knows himself. But few men, it would appear, know themselves more, and less, than Terence Alan Milligan. In James Joyce's *Ulysses* the pragmatically English Mr Haines tells the young Stephen Dedalus:

> *We feel in England that we have treated you rather unfairly. It seems history is to blame.*[2]

Milligan's sense of history is acute. It is the long memory sort – of injustice to his race. The Irish are the poor, down-trodden, yet indomitable-never-to-be-vanquished victims of Haines-like victors, 'bursting with money and indigestion'.

To Milligan, his people are kind and hard done by. He would have agreed with Joyce's reply to Wyndham Lewis when the latter said he thought that the Irish were 'pugnacious'. Slowly, deliberately, Joyce told him:

> *That's not been my experience – a very gentle race.*

Nor does Milligan see any conflict of loyalties in being a member of the British Armed Forces and a critic of her role in Ireland. None of his family had a soft passage in the army. His father, Leo, they used to call 'an Irish cunt' because he had a very strong Irish accent when he was young:

He took up boxing, and then proceeded to beat the shit out of those who jeered him.

But nobody could ever question the family's constancy; if they took your shilling you got a fair twelve penn'orth in return. A fair day's killing for a fair day's pay.

Milligan is very conscious of his Irishry. All his countrymen are. No less could be expected from a people whose very future, until quite recently, has been the past. His seemingly genuine outrage in 1971, therefore, at being denied a British passport seems, expressed now, to be the quintessence of procrastination. He believes that it relegated him to the position of being stateless. Only five years previously, on 22nd April, 1965, he had been a guest at a Buckingham Palace dinner party when, with his second wife, Paddy, he had brought gifts that his children, Laura, Sean, and Sile, had spent weeks making for the Queen. And now he was being thought of as some sort of subversive!

They never informed me in writing, nor was there any publication in the papers.

He found out only by accident. He took his passport to be renewed, and the passport officer asked, 'How long have you had this?' Spike told him to look at the front; and was then told that he was in illegal possession of the document and they took it back.

What puzzles Milligan most is why nobody ever asked him for a passport on his way through North Africa with the Eighth Army, or when being bombed at Salerno, or while crawling on his belly at Monte Cassino.

Having been denied British nationality, he went down to the Irish Embassy and asked if he could join the Republic. They told him, 'God yes, Spike – we're awful short of our own people.' They gave him a jar of Jameson's and a passport, and Spike Milligan has never been happier with himself. He keeps stirring it up just for the sake of stirring it up. He keeps asking the Foreign Office what are his alternatives, his real alternatives.

And they say, 'Well, you could become a Hindu. . .'

He has but to write to the High Commissioner in India. Spike says it's a good job the British Army wasn't on the moon when he was born. 'Imagine me a moonie?'

Despite his annoyance with the passports office, Milligan could never deny that he, or any of his, ever thought of themselves as other than Irish; and Spike – only the second of the family to be born outside the country – is even more bitterly Irish than his ancestors. He used to wonder when he was a kid why his dad was so naturally intelligent:

Why was he so good-looking? And was this the reason the English cartoonists used to caricature the Irish as pigs?

Not that either Spike or his father could be serious for long even about something as important as their cherished heritage. Leo used to tell him a story about an uncle who was only five feet six and a member of the Irish Guards. A guardsman? Impossible! Not to the father of the future Goon. 'He lied,' said Leo, 'about his height.'

But, for all the self-mockery, the history is always there: always to blame. Unsure of whether to accept an invitation to the wedding of Prince Charles and Princess Diana, he rebukes his mother for trying to make him attend:

Don't talk to me about England. After all the English did on us. We're Irish, aren't we? Didn't your own grandmother tell you so. What have we to do with England?

Because personal-friendship is less remote than nationality, Spike went to the wedding. He is genuinely fond of the Prince of Wales and his parents. He likes Princess Diana. The royal family has always asked after him kindly and Spike finds it hard to dislike people who are nice to him. He is not snobbish about the upper classes and refuses to disbar people because of their privilege or wealth. He swears that friends like Paul Getty and Prince Charles can sometimes feel as lonely as anybody else.

And yet he feels that his friend, Getty, dispenses charity disproportionately:

Paul gave twenty thousand pounds to help the miners, but he thought that the M.C.C. were in need of five million pounds. I'm as fond of cricket as the next but that's making sport too important altogether.

It's the class-consciousness of the man that enables him to be a classless intellectual. He may live on the edge of his thoughts but Milligan's mind is very much his own. He changes it quite frequently, and his thinking is never dependent on national, political, or party considerations:

Yes, I change my mind. Who was it said, 'A good idea must give way to a better one . . .'?

The first of the thoroughly modern Milligans to leave home was great-grandfather Michael. Spike, an obsessive archivist, says:

He was posted to Woolwich and, almost immediately, sent to Newfoundland where he arrived on 8th June, 1835.

At twenty-six Michael married Elizabeth Louise Kennedy and they came back to Woolwich with their first child, Elizabeth Mary, on 7th October, 1844. He was transferred to the Adjutants Detachment, Dublin, in 1846. But the fields, white with mushrooms, forecast disaster to the staple food of Ireland, the potato. During that year Irish members of the armed forces could not be trusted to shoot down their starving fellow countrymen. Spike Milligan's great-grandfather found himself on the move again.

1847 and the tenth anniversary of Queen Victoria's accession to the throne was not the best time to test a poor man's loyalty to the Empire. The mushrooms hadn't lied. It was the year of 'The Great Hunger' when the potato crop rotted in the ground, and the grain harvest was plentiful only to be exported – sold off by absentee landlords to the highest foreign bidders. Emigration, if hardly a panacea, was at least a way of saving half a loaf, of getting the poor out of Ireland, England, Scotland and Wales.

Every day coffin ships were filled with starving emigrants, while merchantmen left the same British ports overflowing with produce that the people were unable to purchase. The poor English, Scots and Welsh suffered every bit as much as their Irish counterparts, but they were the silent majority and few folk kept records of their misery. 1847 saw the beginning of the decline in the population of Ireland from close on ten million people to less than four million today both north and south of the divide.

In Michael Milligan's part of Ireland housing conditions were:

wretched beyond words . . . Furniture was a luxury; the inhabitants of Tullahobagley, County Donegal, numbering about nine thousand, had in 1837 only 10 beds, 93 chairs and 243 stools between them. Pigs slept with their owners, manure heaps

choked doors, sometimes even stood inside; the evicted and un-
employed put roofs over ditches, burrowed into banks, existed
in bog-holes.[3]

The Irish members of the armed forces were dispatched to the four corners of the earth so as they would not get into rebellious mischief. Michael Patrick Milligan was sent to Newfoundland where Michael John was born in 1848. Followed by Elanour Margaret in 1850; after whom came Spike's grandfather, William Patrick, on 5th August, 1851.

Michael Pat's early life in the army must have been fraught with difficulties. Because he didn't have a word of English, this Gaelic-speaking Irishman was regarded in army records of the period as being 'an illiterate'.

But then if poverty is the spur of the rich, the wealth of indigence is expedience. Michael taught himself to read and write in English, which accomplishment Spike thought so great that he remains angry to this day that no record of his great-grandfather's achievement remains. Spike told me:

All his documents were signed with an X, you see . . . for a long time in his army paybook 'ex-ex-ex-ex-ex'. And bit by bit he started to write the word 'Milligan', and it starts off very crude and becomes much better. . . .

Then, as if he had been too serious for too long, Spike laughed and said that when he was little he used to ask his father why the Milligans wrote their names in 'joined-up writing' while most of the soldiers spelled theirs with an X. His father told him about another relation who was asked to spell the word 'paint', but he refused to do so until they named a colour.

Michael's home county of Donegal is bordered on its southern side by counties Leitrim and Sligo. Sligo, where Yeats first knew his 'Indomitable Irishry'. And indeed 'indomitable' Michael proved to be, for this one-time 'illiterate' time-server rose to the rank of Gunnery-Sergeant even before he and Elizabeth Louise Kennedy made a home in Newfoundland.

Spike thinks that on his great-grandmother's side he might be related to the Kennedys, and that amuses him greatly. However, Jacqueline Kennedy's efforts to be French petit-bourgeois in preference to her Irish ancestry amuses him even more:

Imagine John F, and old Joe and Honey Fitz, doing their damn-

*dest to come from Wexford so as to prove that their past entitled
them to a future, and this Greek widow wants to be descended
from shop-keepers! My past is the only thing that has ever
made my present worthwhile.*

About his mother's side he's not too sure. He just doesn't
know. Ask and he'll simply say that he's glad he has a lot of Irish
blood in him. He'll tell you that his mother's father was English
and called Alfred Kettleband. Maybe, he'll say, it's German 'Kei-
telbund'. His mother's mother, a Miss Ryan:

*married a Scot, John Burnside, and they had this daughter,
Margaret Flora. Half Irish and half Scots.*

Spike has no room in the family cupboard for skeletons. His
honesty is both alarming and disarming. His great-grandfather
on the Kettleband side, a corporal, was thrown out of the army:

. . . for stealing a comrade's overcoat and selling it.

He doesn't remember that particular ancestor with fondness, and
not because he was a thief, for Spike revels in disclosing family
light-fingeredness. About Leo's scams when quarter-master in
India, he says:

*My old man lived the life of a gentleman on sergeant's pay.
Anything that wasn't nailed down was fair game. You know,
he drank champagne because beer cost money! A photograph of
Michael Milligan taken from a daguerreotype I have included
in* Adolf Hitler: My Part in His Downfall. *Oh God, he was
pure Irish!*

After Michael's daughter, Soraya Anne, was born at Woolwich
in 1854, Michael was transferred to the Antrim Military Artillery
at Carrickfergus Castle. It was here that Anne Jane Milligan was
born in 1857. She attended the only Catholic school in Carrickfergus, St Nicholas, which, adds Milligan with obvious
relish, 'is still there'.

Michael retired with the following reference from his O.C.
which said that he had known 'Corporal Milligan of the 3rd
Battalion of the Royal Artillery for nearly two years in my company . . . and he's still sober'.

It was grandfather William Patrick Milligan who eventually
returned to Yeats Country. But Sligo in the nineteenth century
was nearly as poverty-stricken as Donegal. Famine and eviction

were the order of the day. Nor was the hunger due to the wrath of God as had been the Christian message when the potato crops were hit by blight in 1847.

Commissary General, Sir Randolph Routh, wrote from Sligo, on 14th September, 1847, that when 'the fields were teeming with crops . . . it is impossible there can be this total want, this extinction of every supply in the midst of harvest'.

If history is indeed to blame then blame on it also the bitterness of folk who have always held, with Robert Burns, that 'The rank is but the guinea's stamp'. Spike Milligan says that like Bernard Shaw he could never take a knighthood off the English. Could never take anything from them.

> *After all, they took everything else off me – including the family farm. Then, according to my grandmother, Miss Ryan, they burned the bloody cottage to the ground around their heads. That's no story. That's history that came down through the family, the bastards.*

Two Mercenary Mendicants

*The greatest of evils
and the worst of crimes, is poverty.*

George Bernard Shaw, preface to *Major Barbara*

William Patrick Milligan, much to his father's annoyance, joined
the Royal Artillery in 1869. The army, Michael believed, was a
last resort and should not be entered lightly. Truth is, Spike's
grandfather was running away from a paternity suit in Carrickfergus. Spike told me:

> *Granddad was a sooner – the sooner he got out of Ireland, the
> better. That's why he didn't join the army in Belfast.*

And that was how William Patrick became the exception to
the rule – an Irishman who soldiered for reasons other than abject
poverty. His father had done well in the forces. He had made a
comfortable life for his family in Carrickfergus, and had saved
enough to set up house in County Sligo when the army told him
that he and Louise would live on half pay. He was heart-broken
when his favourite son joined up. Spike speaks as if he's looking
over his antecedents' shoulders:

> *OK, so some of them had to join the army, but only if the need
> arose. The Milligans' first duty was to Ireland – we all knew
> that. We were reared in that knowledge. Mother now, she's a
> different case altogether. She worships royalty. And I say,
> 'What the hell did they ever do for you?' and she replies, 'Oh
> it's a great honour.' But of course they did damn all for
> anybody, indeed their ancestors beat the shit out of us.*

In three years at Woolwich, the army trained Spike's grandfather in the trade of wheeler: they gave him a badge, an extra
few pence a week and Spike gave the badge to his brother, Desmond. William Patrick arrived in the East End of London at
about the same time that William Booth, unsuccessful pawnbrok-
ing son of an unsuccessful builder, was preaching the American

evangelical solution to poverty: 'Bang the drum till thy kingdom come.'

Does Blessed Margaret really know what Victorian values were worth? Has she ever read a book – I mean one with more words than figures?

The Victorian years, when Jesus and jingoism went hand in hand through the infant Empire, must have been good for Booth and William Patrick Milligan. Oh happy days! When funerals were among the simple pleasures of the poor, the demise of the mighty was occasion for public wailing. What with the death of Albert, the assassination of Lincoln, your man in the street must have been in his element. Certainly William Patrick would have been glad in 1872 to get away to the salubrious quiet of Malta.

Soldiers, the world's first commuters. Willie was barely a year in the Mediterranean before he returned to Britain in 1873. As a wheelright in the 9th Brigade he was stationed at Dover Castle where he met and courted Lizzie Higgins. They were married on 2nd April, 1878. Spike thinks:

Grandfather must have been a very fit man to keep granny happy and the gun carriages moving.

Lizzie had three children in four years. Milligan says that Michael John was born in 1879, to be followed by Kathleen Elizabeth the next year and then William Bernard, who was born in 1882 at Gravesend. Spike is lost in amazed admiration:

They didn't stop, did they? And what about all that moving around!

A grand year for Milligans surely.

But what about 1885? Captain Charles Cunningham Boycott, who had made his name synonymous with secular excommunication, was happy in 1885 to be taking up employment in England. And, while Captain Boycott was trying out his new career as Suffolk bailiff . . .? Spike says:

The reverend Strickland of the West Indies was writing a letter of thanks to Sergeant William Patrick Milligan for singing in the church choir. Benediction for the Barbados.

William Patrick was no fool. He knew that the best protection an Irishman could have just then was a khaki uniform and an army pay-book. Corduroy was a poor tartan where the want-ads all said, 'No Irish Need Apply'. William Patrick Milligan was well off. Spike believes that the real heroes and heroines of life are the fathers who make a living when all the odds are against them and the mothers who never give up the fight for a square meal for the kids.

Carlyle says:

> No great man lives in vain. The history of the world is but the biography of great men.[1]

But Irish history is no biography of great men. All our great men were Anglo-Irish and, until the French, Anglo-Alien. It is the story of them and us. History to the Irish is as important as is land to the Russian peasant. There is no possible way that Irishmen like Milligan will be understood without knowing what historical forces motivated their very thinking.

Sometimes history gets in the way of progress. Spike believes that the British press set about holding the Irish race and all things Irish up to ridicule simply because they wanted to sell newspapers. But incidents like Tonypandy and the Highland Clearances did happen.

However, politics, poverty, and pianos apart, better a mercenary than a mendicant. William Milligan was to be envied, however much he might have hated the travelling. Spike told me that in 1882 his grandparents boarded the SS *Bolivard*, Portsmouth, for a colonial posting and, on 12th December that same year, they were shipwrecked off the Barbados, where on the 18th August, 1884, one child, William Bernard, died.

It might not keep infant mortality at bay but Sergeant William Patrick Milligan's uniform meant, at the very least, a roof, a bed, and bread.

On 17th August, 1888, William Patrick Marmaduke was born, and taken for baptism to St Patrick's in Barbados. Spike's father, Leo Alphonso, was born two years later on 13th April, at either number 5 or 6, Holborn Street, in the County of Sligo. William took his youngest son to the cathedral to have him christened Percy Marmaduke, but the priest said:

> 'Oh God, that's not really a good Irish Catholic name.' So they named him after the current Pope.

He was the so-called 'Workers Pope', Leo XIII, who enjoyed, at the time, the kind of 'liberal' notoriety that came to John XXIII almost three quarters of a century later. The Pope's name didn't do a great deal for Leo Milligan's Catholicism. Spike thinks that his father grew up to be a daylight atheist.

William Patrick Milligan was discharged from the army in 1895, and two years later he arrived in Poplar in the East End of London with a reference from John Keenan of Sligo which said that he had known the 'late' Sergeant William Milligan for seven years:

> . . . *during which time I've always found him sober.*

With references to spare, and each one testifying to abstemious habits and a fear of God, he came to live in England. He soon found employment as a part-time caretaker in Grosvenor Buildings, Manisty Street, Poplar. According to Spike, his grandfather was neither industrious nor teetotal.

> *It was his job to see that all the gas-lamps were lit at night on the landings of these early Victorian apartment blocks. So, he used to go downstairs and drink Jameson's and then kick the arses off his boys and they'd run over all these buildings – there were about six of them setting light to all these gas-lamps. The thing was that the first one back got paid. Some bloody rush! Nearly killed themselves trying to light the lamps!*

Spike says that William could talk anybody, except his children, into doing anything:

> *He persuaded the manager of the Queen's Palace of Varieties, Poplar, that he knew more about the theatre than Sir Henry Irving and, before long, he was in charge of the scenery dock.*

The stage door of the Queen's was almost opposite the back door of his house. In 1903, when he was barely thirteen years of age, Spike's father, Leo, got a job as a screen-puller. He rubbed shoulders with the famous – Fred Karno, Chaplin, Stan Laurel, Marie Lloyd. . . .

And the rest of the Milligans worked as 'supers' and thought themselves 'theatre people'. They got to know a lot about English music hall but not a great deal about drama; indeed Spike thought that his father knew less about theatre then most:

> He didn't know a thing. You see, he was ignorant. He finished
> schooling when he was about twelve. And he had no knowledge
> of Irish literature at all. His father had taken him away from
> Sligo to Britain and he became enamoured of the theatre
> because the buildings he lived in backed onto the old Queen's
> Theatre in Poplar. Gone now.

Leo Alphonso saved enough money to pay for lessons at Stead-man's Dancing Academy. But, apart from them earning pocket money after school, William Patrick wasn't too keen about having a bunch of thespians for a family. Spike says that his father could dance or sing a song as well:

> I think, in my darkest memory, that he told me that his father
> also did Irish step-dancing. At Steadman's Dancing Academy
> he fell in love with the international dancer – Nijinsky's prima
> ballerina – Lydia Sokolova, when she was still Hilda Munnings
> from Poplar.

Leo was mad about the stage and Spike says he was born to be a trooper. He came from a family who should have been on the stage. His mother was a very fine singer and piano-player. She was, like Leo, a dancer. Given all this, Milligan thinks that the prevailing Irish attitude where, if you couldn't get a job you joined the army, was a form of madness. You could have a clear conscience learning how to kill people, but the stage was definitely out:

> So my father was pushed into the army as a boy soldier at the
> age of fourteen!

Young Leo won a talent contest as a 'Coon Singer and Dancer' and was given a week's work at the Woolwich Garrison Theatre. Spike has the original contract and the original playbill with his father's name on it. He called himself 'Leo Gann' because 'Milligan' would have been too big and therefore the print would have been smaller.

Not long afterwards, Leo Alphonso was posted to India, as a private in the Royal Artillery. William Patrick became stage manager of the Queen's. This was cementing a new tradition since William's father Michael, said Spike, had been:

> hall-keeper at the Theatre Royal in Glasgow round about 1887.
> Michael never got back to Ireland; he died in 1892 at 36,
> West Russell Street, Glasgow.

In the summer of 1913 Leo came across Flo Kettleband. She was singing at Mass in Poona. At that time she seems to have been intent on pursuing a career in music – marriage was not high on her list of priorities. But the boy from Sligo courted well and was only biding his time. It came the following June with the assassination of an almost redundant pair of royals, Francis Ferdinand and his wife, at Sarajevo.

Convinced that he would be sent to the front at the outbreak of hostilities, Leo persuaded Flo to agree to a civil wedding ceremony on the understanding that the marriage would later be solemnized by the church at the earliest possible opportunity. They were married by licence in Poona in September, 1914, just a month after the war in Europe had started. The ceremony took place hurriedly in room 13 of the Poona Hotel in front of a registrar. Flo's father was waiting outside and he chased Leo through Poona Markets on a bike, flinging rocks as he pursued the honeymoon couple:

> *Father told his tonga driver to drive like mad. The ensuing scene is straight from Hollywood. There's this Max Sennet bicycle chase going on through India, just crazy. In the end, my father called out that if her father desisted from throwing rocks, he'd have the marriage solemnized at a Catholic chapel before taking my mother to bed.*

Three Yes Surrender!

> *I have ever hated*
> *all nations, professions and*
> *communities, and all my love*
> *is towards individuals.*
>
> Swift to Pope, 1725

An old fisherman says:

> *Never go to sea. Put an oar on your back. Start walking away*
> *from the ocean. Go far enough into the country until somebody*
> *asks, 'What's that you've got on your shoulder?' Drop your*
> *anchor there.*

Ernest Hemingway thinks, in *A Farewell to Arms*, that the
way to end war is to walk away from it. After the Athenian dis-
asters in Sicily, Aristophanes' Lysistrata encouraged the women
to do a deal with their men – sex for peace, make love not war.
Spike Milligan's cure is to send all the soldiers into battle
similarly dressed, or naked, or with their hands up.

> *Let nobody tell friend from foe. Wear drab uniforms. Wave no*
> *flags. Flags and uniforms make men proud. Pride goes before a*
> *fall, everybody knows that.*

Spike's war would be like the hurley match played between
two Irish teams, in the middle of which the winning side decides
it is time to go home but the referee tells the other side to play
on, and eventually they score the equalizing goal.

That, he says, is what should happen in war: the people should
just give up and go home. If soldiers kissed each other they would
be too embarrassed to fight. As soon as they asked him to wear a
uniform, he wanted to say, 'That's dangerous,' and if they asked
what was dangerous about it, he wanted to tell them that soldiers
needed anonymity to feel safe.

He frequently tells the story of how, in the early forties, some
dejected German soldiers, wishing to resign from the war, ap-

proached him. Milligan's officer had his back to them. Spike reported:

> '*There are some Germans here, sir, they have their hands above their heads.*' '*Ask them what they want, corporal.*' '*They wish to surrender, sir.*' '*Tell them we don't have the facilities. Tell them to go away.*'

And when they insisted on turning themselves in, the officer shooed away the would-be surrenderers as one would scatter a clutch of chickens.

Spike's unshakeable belief in the innate goodness of his fellow man is all-pervading. This very gentle child of the regiment seems to have a childlike faith in his fellow man. But Milligan knows that to acknowledge war is to make it a fact. Close your eyes and the guns cannot see you.

Leo Alphonso hated war, but he loved uniforms. He enjoyed nothing better than playing the soldier on the stage. The newly weds did a double act as 'Gwen Gorden and Leo Gann'. The army brass closed a military eye to the fact that the duo were appearing in professional theatres for professional money, playing a comedy song and dance act in a sketch written by Leo called 'Fun Round the Sentry Box'.

They appeared in, among other venues, the Bombay Palace Theatre of Varieties and, while appearing on the professional circuit, Leo mounted regimental shows for the entertainments committee in Poona.

The army chose to ignore the part-time soldiering of this forerunner to E.N.S.A. because, Spike believes, his father was very good:

> *That's how he got so much leave. He'd do lots of work for the troops – concerts and other shows. He was in good blood with the officers – especially the colonels. So whenever he said, 'I've been given a booking to go to Bombay for a fortnight, will you give me fourteen days' leave?', they'd say, 'Of course,' because when he came back he'd do shows for the soldiers, gratis.*

Talking with Spike about those times in Poona, one is ever conscious of the non-political nature of army conversation among the lower ranks. Soldiers seldom asked the reason why. Why they were in India, or Egypt, or Africa. They were workers in khaki overalls, brought to the Punjab on the whims of petty

Indian princes or the merchant princes of Lipton's and the British East India Company whose agents learned to master oriental custom. By treaty, bribery, annexation and all sorts of skulduggery, the commercial empire spread throughout the sub-continent.

But this colony was not Ireland. No question here of dispossessing the indigenous people and planting the place with loyal Scots. The people of India were needed by everybody from prince to planter. Necessary if only to remember that.

The sahib's most difficult chore was to learn that a *palkee-wallah* was one of those to carry him about on the litter. That a *punkah-coolie* took care of his horse. A *khitmutgar* waited on him at table. That an *ayah* took care of his wife's needs while the *mussalchi* washed her dirty dishes. Oh yes, and there was of course the *mehtar* to sweep up after the lot of them.

The British Empire threw up new B-movie heroes, merchant warriors like Gordon and Clive. The Victorians sang songs about the first yuppies, Henry Lawrence, John Nicholson and Henry Havelock, who believed in the superiority of civilization.

Yet, sjamboks apart, new orders need slaves and, in the case of India, only the indigenous population filled the bill. But bread breeds impertinence: fear of independence forced the merchant army into an accommodation with the Indian upper classes after eighteen months of the most bitter rebellion in the history of the British Empire.

It is said that the ferocity of the Indian Mutiny surprised the Indians as much as it did the British. The new British Army in India was shocked at the extent of the hatred they generated. From places like Lucknow, Cawnpore and Delhi, the fiercest fighting made the colonials second-best in the war games. The British establishment was learning that there is a price to be paid for empire-building.

And, as if that were not aggravation enough, the Indian-born English were becoming a force with which to be reckoned. They, and the end of direct control by the City of London, marked the beginnings of Anglo-Indian rule: the Raj. A totally accidental and nationless conception, but without which Britain would never have been able to hold on to India after independence.

Indeed, long before 1948, the only way that the British Army of occupation could hold the sub-continent was by creating (to some extent artificially) the class society which evolved naturally over the centuries in the British Isles. The Raj, in turn, spawned an Indian Civil Service, an Indian Army and all the reforms that follow from quasi home rule. And the Raj felt even more superior to the indigenous Indians than did the foreign-born crusaders. Familiarity breeding contempt? Spike says:

> *I never saw anything like the way the natives were treated, and yet they were supposed to smile when beaten. It wouldn't have been the Irish! No bejazes, we would have kicked the bastards from Poona to kingdom come.*

Nor was Spike exaggerating. In 1915 we find a former professor of English at the Presidency college in Calcutta writing, in a handbook to advise Indians who 'might expect to have dealings with the British somewhere above the menial level', that to chew betel or anything else is not in English society considered to be polite.

They must not use the words 'stomach' or 'bowels', and woe to those who thought that belly was another name for the abdomen. Even etiquette seemed to be in the hands of the accountants, since the message was:

> *Transact all the business of the table quietly and gently. Do not eat quickly or ravenously and never smack your lips. . . .*[1]

Small wonder that Spike boasts of having eaten curry with his hands. But patronage is insidious. Milligan remembers that it was a question of being strangers in their own land:

> *In England our troops were treated like natives: as they were not native to India, they were treated better. So our troops learned to treat the Indians as natives. They got the shit beaten out of them by the ordinary soldiers. They were called 'wogs' and 'half-chats' and 'chi-chis'. All words concocted by the British Indian Army.*

Of course this was to be expected for, with the likelihood of insurrection in every part of India since the end of the nineteenth century, it was psychologically necessary to make the middle and lower-middle class Indians feel inferior.

And, from table etiquette to more general social behaviour. Included in the handbook was a section which might well have been named, 'How to mind your place'. Indians must learn to 'tolerate criticism' and not be 'over-sensitive' to it. 'Englishmen are apt on occasion to be somewhat rough-and-ready in what they say and do' but they didn't mean it. So Indians were not to:

> . . . convert a hasty word or what is intended only for jest into a deadly insult.[2]

Yet maybe the most pretentious, most arrogant, most patronizing instruction of all is given to the English and deals with the native's 'self-respect': to his prestige, *izzat*, which could be translated as self-respect.

> While it is a cardinal virtue in handling men, whether in the East or in the West, not to reprove them in the presence of others who are subordinates, it is particularly the case in India.[3]

The British colonists were nothing if not condescending. Thus in 1914 we find H. N. C. Campbell, Master of the Madras Hunt, begging his subscribers not to ride over crops or cross the middle of the fields and make lanes all through the paddy: not to damage the crop while it is ready for cutting or is lying cut on the ground, or ride over garden crops or seed-beds.

Probably most entertaining of all was an evening of 'High Cockalorum', where at a party the guests would line out as two rugger teams. One team would form itself into a tight scrum and the opposing side would attempt to break the scrum by jumping on it. What could be more enjoyable? Better still, a guest was armed with cards which could hardly be described as visiting cards. They were probably known as 'Morning-after-the-night-before' cards. They were ready-made apologias for any conceivable (or indeed inconceivable) breach of etiquette, from 'Excessive destruction of furniture' to 'Striking host with bottle'!

The mind boggles. 'Excessive destruction of furniture'? What amount of breakages were acceptable? Nothing the officers did ever surprised Spike:

> Officers and gentlemen? Screwing the servants and each other's wives.

There were always two armies in India. As in Ireland and every other part of the Empire, the Liptons and the Clives cut costs by the judicious use of a central pool of domestic cannon fodder. Less than a third of the occupying army was British, and the Raj found that the way to keep the native soldiers loyal was to draw recruits, not only from particular races but, wherever possible:

> from the same clans and villages; with sons following fathers,
> and nephews following their uncles, so that, over the years, a
> strong tradition of kinship developed within each regiment . . .
> The sense of family was further stressed by the way in which
> each regiment lived in cantonments as a self-contained
> community, cutting itself off from the outside world.[4]

The Milligans had, from 1837, followed the same path in the Royal Artillery. As Spike says, his family, like all the British Other Ranks (BORs), were better off than their counterparts in the Indian Army. But the native troops must have been very badly off indeed.

The privileged, blissfully unaware that the mother country was fighting for her life, were, no doubt, enjoying 'High Cockalorum' as the first Milligan went off to war.

On 7th November, 1914, Corporal L. Milligan, 17th Poona Division, landed at the Persian Gulf. Another Indian Division which had already arrived, escorted by the *Ocean* and the sloops *Espiegle* and *Odin*, established an entrenched position at Abadan. Spike's research reveals that:

> The six Poona Divisions sailed in 1914 but, as it says in the
> book The Forgotten War, all of them arrived in dribs and
> drabs. My father wrote about the landings to his father and the
> address was, 'Mr W. Milligan, 489, Manistry Street, Poplar.'
> He was, I think, according to a photograph I have, under
> canvas at a holding camp outside Bombay. . . .

In December the *Ocean* was withdrawn to the Dardanelles, but by a rapid and well-planned stroke the troops, supported by the two sloops, *Espiegle* and *Odin*, took command of the Persian Gulf to ensure control of the oil-fields.

Meanwhile, the 17th Poona Division was on its way to Mesopotamia where it planned to take on the Turks on their home ground. Leo's letter to his father says:

> Anchored mid-stream. Ferried to the shore by bielams (Arab
> Dhows). Battery expected to be in action for the Battle of
> Shaibin (Boadicea Wood). By dawn only three guns and two
> wagons ready to move. Bitterly cold with cavalry escort moving
> to the battle ground.

Spike is immensely proud of his father's achievements. He is immensely proud of his father. He is particularly proud that his father, like his father and his father before him, kept records of what they considered important. Small wonder that Spike Milligan knows how to choose his words. What Joyce thought of as his 'epiphanies', Leo called 'calendars':

> *Let me see . . . 1916? 1917? . . . I'm an archivist by nature. I've actually got lyrics he wrote. . . . Like me, believe it or not, he was promoted in the field. That must be some kind of distinction, don't you think? Where are we? What bit did you ask me about? Ah, yes, here we are now. . . . 'April, 1915, two weeks' action in Shaibin. 14th April, 1915, promoted sergeant in the field. . . .'*

Hollywood has been blamed for glorifying war, but it would have to really exaggerate to outdo the newspapers and penny-dreadfuls of Grub Street. There was the 'calm, cool, unflappable' General Townshend directing the most flamboyant amphibious battle outside Kurnah, before joining with the Royal Indian Marines to chase the 'treacherous Turks' up the Euphrates at the head of a flotilla of gunboats brought specially from England. Was this the same battle for Mesopotamia which is remembered nowadays as one of the bloodiest of World War One?

And, despite the action he must have seen, Leo's 'calendars' are remarkably free of vainglory. They are, in their matter-of-factness, almost anti-heroic:

> *18th June, 1915. He says, 'Field hospital. Worst case was four soldiers who travelled from Kirkuk to Ahvez by ambulance. Bounced over the sandhills with the dysentery of the patient above dripping down on me. . . .'*

Spike disputes the accuracy of the calendars for he cannot believe that an orderly would allow one wounded man to drip all over another. He is sceptical about the truth of his father's statement that, after twenty-nine days, the doctor diagnosed Leo's illness as a 'mild enteric':

> *I can't believe that. I put 'absurd!' Father also said it was diagnosed as inflammation of the soft palate. I think he invented this. He was a bugger for this.*

Spike's soul comes from his father and he is fiercely protective of Leo's memory. He is fearful that history may construe exaggeration as deliberate falsehood. He hides his father behind himself in much the same way that he hid himself in a bunch of Goons, for he believes, as Swift knew, that 'Satire is a sort of glass wherein beholders do generally discover everybody's face but their own'. Thus the son makes fun even of his own explanations of his father's condition:

> *Possibly it was malaria, because later, after the war, he talks of going down with repeated bouts of malaria. He says, 'On discharge from hospital I had a good meal that nearly fucking killed me! Mobilized base depot for three days. Returned to hospital'.*

Is this the Mesopotamian butchery about which historians have written so luridly? Are these the same graveyards of the British, Serbs, Australians and Turks that people talk of to show us the evil futility of war? Was Leo writing about something so awful that to treat it less than pragmatically would have been too painful? Is it like father like son? Spike later told me how it was when he arrived in Salerno on 23rd September, 1943:

> *Conquerors? Liberators? No, we didn't go to Italy as conquerors or liberators. We went there shit-scared and that's the truth.*

Four Daddy's Dressed in Khaki

If England is the land of our fathers,
India is the land of our mothers.

Quoted by Geoffrey Moorhouse, *India Britannica*

Nationality-wise, Leo Milligan had the best of two worlds: he could be British without being English and Irish without being British. He might have resented 'them' seeing his son as Anglo-Indian; he might have been hurt at the implied inferiority, but he would have seen Spike's efforts to obtain a British passport as little more than a 'bit of crack', all part of that Swiftian Irishry we might have called 'Milligan's Wake'! Spike knows damned well that a lot changed between 1900 and 1971.

Being Irish is full-time and complicated enough. Spike's people are a mass of contradictions. The Irish, always conscious of their country as a nation, are not the most homogeneous people in the world. Nobody loves the Irish like themselves, or hates them more than each other. Race is hardly the collective term for a group of persons recognizable by little other than their own individuality.

The collective Spike says, 'My country right or wrong.' He stood on Arbour Hill in Dublin where the leaders of the 1916 Rising are buried. It was a lonely autumn day with just a few leaves going round and an old man sweeping, and Spike suddenly realized that he was so Irish:

> *I tell you I started to cry. To cry at these men. I thought, 'My God did they really die for me like Jesus?' They actually did and they were young.*

He and Peter Sellers went to see a film about Ireland. And when they were walking home, Sellers asked, 'Aren't you proud to be Irish?' And Milligan answered, 'Yes, but not because of the film. I'm just proud to be Irish. I think we're different.'

On the other hand there is the first-person-singular Spike who boasts that the name Milligan has so many variants that the family might have sired the entire race. There were the Mulligans and the O'Mealagains, Malachy who wore the collar of gold, and Molyneaux from France. Even Stanley Baldwin was but the English of Milligan because the name means 'The Small–Tonsured One'.

When Dr Johnson told the Bishop of Killaloe that 'The Irish are a fair people; they never speak well of one another', he might have added that many of them seldom speak well of anybody. To some, like Mayor Daley of Chicago, nigger-bashing seems to be the favourite sport of the Paddy who was 'born with a potato in his head'.

Leo's racism appalled and amused his son. Spike saw it as fury signifying nothing. His mother and father would call the natives half-jacks or coons and Milligan will plead that everybody is a bit like that. He cites instances. Like the time he was in Glasgow digs where he stayed with a Mrs O'Brien and her family, 'in Sauciehall Street – those big stone tenements'. One evening, Mrs O'Brien – a huge mountain of a woman – was serving out the supper and she said to the black trumpet player, 'Mr Wilkins, what kind of nigger are you?' 'Jamaica,' Dave replied. 'Ah,' she said, 'so yer that kind of a nigger.'

Milligan thinks there's nothing malicious in ignorance; he believes that to wound, you must intend to hurt:

> She wasn't racist; she only knew the word 'nigger'.

In July, 1915, Leo Milligan was transferred to the military hospital at Poona. This made it much easier for his wife to visit him. Because the temperature could soar to 120 degrees Fahrenheit in the Indian shade, the British created rest stations in, for example, the 'cool' districts of Darjeeling, Simla, Muree, Mussourie and Nainital on the slopes of the Himalayas. Unlike most soldiers' wives, Flo refused to make for the hills during the hot months, and not just because her husband was in hospital. Years later, Leo wrote to Spike:

> Your mother always refused to be parted from me during the hot weather and insisted on staying behind to take her place in the Friday night concerts – which were, of course, a great success.

On 19th August, 1915 – to the great satisfaction of Spike's grandfather – Leo and Flo's marriage was solemnized at St

Patrick's Roman Catholic Church, Poona. Spike is still surprised, amused, and a little proud that the chapel was named after Ireland's patron saint:

> *Would you believe that they gave the cathedral an Irish name!*
> *St Patrick's! Right in the middle of a Hindu area!*

It would seem that because Leo Milligan was attached to an 'English' regiment of the British Army he knew little about what was going on in the political world and Ireland in particular. The Royal Artillery was not the same as, say, the Munsters or the Leinsters, or the Dublin Fusiliers. They certainly were not as aware as the Connaught Rangers. I asked Spike if his father had ever talked much about the Easter Rising. But he never had. Not a word. It was as though 1916 had never happened. If Leo knew anything at all about the Irish question he never let on. The real rebel Milligan was Uncle Willie who had lost a leg at Mons.

Willie had been serving with a Protestant regiment, the Enniskillens, and he told Spike that they'd sent him back with a broomstick and a pension of one shilling and one penny per week. Willie came across a grand piano and thought that the odd leg would do better than the broomstick. He hollowed out this piano leg so as to make it lighter, put a leather clamp along the top and tied it to his stump. Deliberately he made it rough so as to keep the trouser leg straight – 'without that his trouser leg looked flapped about, yeh see, but the roughness made it seem as if he'd got a matching leg.'

Then Willie came to Dublin looking for the rebels, and he found Tomas O'Raghailly who used to make grenades for the republicans. Willie discovered that he could fit two grenades into the top of his wooden leg and as an old soldier he could pass through the military cordons without too much trouble:

> *My father told me, 'Two hand-grenades a week he used to*
> *bring to the rebels and all he ever said was, "Jazes Christ, Leo,*
> *but I could have blown me arse up most days of the year."'*

Willie fascinated Spike. He longed to see his own father with the same anarchic outlook as his uncle, and in both *Puckoon* and *The Looney* he seems to combine the characters of Willie and Leo:

Most of the things I do like that bring out the idiot nature of man. That is what I intend. Like Jacques Tati it makes fun of the pompousness of the human race – or sections of it. The human race is always praising itself. It's the nonsense of the whole thing. There are those who want to sentence murderers to death and who would make heroes of people who kill in war – and yet it's the same act, only more so. And man, the gigantic Narcissus, has this constant ridiculous love affair with himself. He's supposed to be modest and yet man is never done praising himself, for ever and ever.

And that leg fascinated Spike. He remembers that Uncle Willie used to put a shoe on the bottom of it. Milligan thinks back, savours the memory and then says with a smile:

He lived and died for Ireland in Ireland, Uncle Willie. Having sold one leg to England for a shilling, he was willing to give the other one to Ireland – free, gratis, for nothing.

But one mystery bothered Spike all his life . . . and, now that Willie's dead and gone, he regrets never having asked him . . . What happened to the piano? He means to say, if 'the bloke' had to play it afterwards, he must have had to go up a ladder! Up a ladder to play a piano!

Milligan loves the past because he can alter his memory of it to suit any mood. The present tends to get in the way because it is meant for the pedantic: the future is a matter of opinion – anybody's. But the past? That's where Milligan is king:

I've wondered about that piano all my life. True as God, sometimes when I'd be doodling I'd find meself drawing pianos at an angle of forty-five degrees. Must have done that to the age of forty. In Q2 I had these false legs on string. I had them across a table and, while I was talking, these legs just went straight up over my head, straight up in the air.

In *Puckoon* the legs of The Milligan seem to lead a life of their own:

'Holy God! Wot are dese den? Eh?' He looked around for an answer. 'Wot are dey?' he repeated angrily.
'Legs.'
'Legs? Legs? Whose legs?'
'Yours.'

'*Mine? And who are you?*'

'*The Author.*'

'*Author? Author? Did you write these legs?*'

'*Yes.*'

'*Well, I don't like dem. I don't like 'em at all. I cauld ha' writted better legs meself. Did you write your legs?*'

'*No.*'

'*Ahhh. Sooo. You got someone else to write your legs, someone who's a good leg-writer, and den you write dis crappy pair of old legs fer me, well mister, it's not good enough. . . . .*'[1]

To Milligan, music is merely an accompaniment for thought. But writing, like his reading, was something he came to by himself. He didn't know there were any rules so he broke them all. Escaping the control of reason? Realism, surrealism; Milliganese: it is totally subconscious, and preconceived only in experience.

He is easily hurt because he lacks some of the overt cynicism of his race. The sardonic need to take most things Irish with a ton of salt is a prerequisite to survival among a people who have been able to take even the cutest of Hollywood Christians by their innocent necks and stuff them full of romantic notions.

So Spike's ideas about the 'old country'. Ah, if only he knew. Ireland was possibly the biggest garrison country of the British Empire and, but for Easter executions, Dublin might still be the brightest jewel in the crown. On Wednesday nights, when the old sweats had been to the Linenhall in Dublin to collect their pensions, the air would ring with songs like, 'The Rose of No Man's Land' and 'The Banks of the Nile' rather than the melodies of revolutionary republicanism.

The idiom of the city people had come straight from the barrack-room, and Dublin kids were far more familiar with words like buckshee, a corruption of the Egyptian *baksheesh*, than with the Irish galore – which really only entered our vocabulary after we met up with the celluloid begorrah speakers from Hollywood.

We sang about the glories of the North-West Passage and the wonders of Kipling's Empire. Only the Anglo-Irish like Yeats and Lady Wilde knew about the sons of Fionn and Cuchullian and the 'Daughters of Lir'. Most of the 'real' Irish were the children of soldiers. My first warning about the nature of stupidity came in the phrase, 'Old soldier old shite – young soldier gobshite.'

The Irish knew then what it was like to be soldiers of the Queen. They shared the same army culture, the same traditions, the same sense of dedication to the same cause. They defended the interests of the crown in whatever country in the world they happened to find themselves. Those who did not agree with them were rebels.

The daughters of soldiers tended to marry the sons of soldiers. The Milligans were no different to anybody else. Flo and Leo were well suited. The Kettlebands were army and they were Catholic. Because they were converts to the true faith they were less tolerant than the Milligans. They were of this rigid, almost Calvinist type of Catholicism, but for all that, Spike's maternal grandparents were Holy Roman Catholic and Apostolic.

Apart from Grandfather Kettleband being a noted trumpeter, Flo and her sister Eileen danced and sang, and Flo played the piano. Hughie Kettleband played the banjo and ukulele and they all worked in the army concerts. Flo still played the professional circuit and, when Leo was healed, they would once again tread the boards as 'Gwen Gorden and Leo Gann'.

After being discharged from military hospital in 1916, Leo was posted to the 77th Battery and in April, while Dublin was in flames, 'Gorden and Gann' were appearing in a concert at the Excelsior Cinema, Kirkee.

An application by Leo for home leave was refused in 1917 and the Milligans probably never knew how lucky they were. In January of that year the German Government extended the scope of its maritime operations by declaring an unrestricted naval blockade of Great Britain: any ships, Allied or neutral, sailing to British ports were to be sunk at sight. It was no idle threat from a power which had for two and a half years held more than half of Europe at bay. In the first six months of 1917 they had already sunk nearly three million tons of British merchant ships.

And Leo was fortunate too not to have been serving any longer under the swashbuckling General Townshend when his 'flamboyant' force was captured by the Turks at Kut-El-Amara, less than a year after Leo had left Mesopotamia ill but victorious.

In Ireland the War of Independence had just begun and, in India, the Besant Home Rule League (founded by the English expatriate, Annie Besant) had already twenty-seven thousand members. They were particularly active in Poona, while other organizations of the Congress Party under native leadership were turning the sub-continent into a sea of agitation.

A dispatch from the Viceroy's office to the new Prime Minister, Lloyd George, read:

> *Gandhi is daily transfiguring the imaginations of masses of ignorant men with visions of an early millenium.*

England in 1917: a nation of shortages and ration coupons, and not the ideal place of convalescence for Flo Milligan or Spike lying speechless in his mother's womb.

In April 1918 Spike Milligan was born in the cantonment at Poona. Leo remembered the occasion in a letter to his son many years later:

> *The 16th of April will be your birthday, you will be forty-nine years old, and in your 50th year the next day. How time flies, it doesn't seem all that long that I watched Father Rudden give you his blessing and pin a wee gold cross on you the day you were born. I made my way on horseback to the hospital and Father Rudden followed on a bicycle, wishing all the time he had a horse.[2]*

Five The Connaught Rangers

We have just enough religion
to make us hate, but not enough to make
us love one another.

Swift

Spike was a delicate child and during his first year his father was worried. Leo was now frequently away from home on tours of duty and, although she had servants to look after the household chores and her sister, Eileen, to give her a hand with the baby, Flo was anything but well. Despite his mother's protests, the family were sent to the cooler climes of Coonor in the Nilgari hills. Spike says:

> *Ever since she had fallen pregnant with me she had been ill.*
> *While she was expecting me in 1917 my mother refused to*
> *leave the hot parts of India. She became very thin and*
> *emaciated. . . .*

But the Nilgari hills didn't do her or her child a lot of good so the army relented. It is possible that Leo had, in fact, been working his devious barrack-room oracle for, in 1919, when his eldest son was thirteen months old, the Milligans were granted six months' home leave and, according to Spike, his father, knowing how the army can bend the rules, went along as a sick bay attendant. Much to the amusement of his son, who swears that Leo was sick all the way himself!

Although the war was over, the navy was wary of unswept mines. As if the mines lived a life of their own, Spike's father thought about them as 'the enemy' and the apprehension, later expressed by his parents, is recalled by Spike in *The Dreaded Batter Pudding Hurler*.

PETER: As an added precaution they travelled on separate
decks and wore separate shoes on different occasions.
SEAGOON: The ship was disguised as a train – to make the

train sea-worthy it was done up to look like a boat and painted to appear like a tram.

SPIKE: . . . All very confusing, really.[1]

Dr Johnson believed that every man is what he reads. In the case of the Milligans he was quite right: they could have come straight out of the pages of *Robinson Crusoe*. Leo, like his father before him, was shipwrecked. The ship under a Scottish skipper went aground at Mayun off the west coast of Aden, with Leo swearing that the captain never drew a sober breath. Spike said that the log for that clear June evening must have read:

> '*Calm night. Perfect sea. Shipwrecked.* . . . '

It was a steamer, says Spike, called the *Erinpura*:

> . . . *and, before we set off, Dad told my mum that to have the name Erin on a ship was a lucky omen. 'Erin,' he told her, 'was the real name for Ireland.' Lucky for him the other 480 passengers didn't know anything about this when they ran aground. Still, I suppose they must have had some luck since they were picked up by a British destroyer, HMS Topaz from Aden, which was patrolling the Red Sea when the passenger ship was abandoned.*

The passengers were taken to Mustapha Barracks in Alexandria and, after living rough in some prison guards huts, they went by the SS *Plessie* to Marseilles. They lived it up at the Château Aygulard and Spike thinks that his father must have adored every minute of that:

> *He loved nice things. How he would have loved my house, 'Monkenhurst' – it's a sort of rather grand house with big fireplaces. He loved lording it – without being a snob. He loved lording it and he loved to smoke a cigar and drink a glass of wine and pretend he was an expert on it.* . . .

In the best traditions of the Irish story-teller, Milligan the seannaice breaks off now and then to give voice to some relevant though not immediately connected thought. When the theme is family the sentiments are ordered in *leit-motiv*. His love for his friends and his relatives is such that he feels he must constantly give expression to it. And, while he recognizes his father's ignorance, he insists on appreciating his intellect:

*Dad may have been ignorant, but he was very intelligent. One
of his favourite sayings was, 'It only happens all the time.' He
was some man. Of course you don't take much notice of your
father when you're young, do you? You're off with other boys
all the time. When he was dying my mother said, 'Shall we call
the priest?' 'No, no. Think of the dibs, dear. Do better than
that, call a bishop.' That was on his death-bed.*

After a month at the Château Aygulard the Milligans went by
cattle truck to Marseilles. Then by train to Le Havre and from
there to Folkestone. For a while they visited Leo's sister, Kathleen, in Sittingbourne, after which they came down to London
to stay with friends in Poplar.

Life in London must have been exciting enough for Leo
during his home leave but he was far too obedient a soldier to
hear a political idea let alone express one. He wouldn't even have
noticed the fanatical oratory of the young Winston begging the
people of the East End to go to war against the Soviet Union,
because Mr Churchill, according to R. K. Webb:

> . . . found fighting the Bolsheviks a stimulus for his hatred of
> socialism in all its forms and for the military instinct that,
> from his earliest days as a soldier, lay very close to the surface
> in his personality.[2]

Good soldier that he was, Leo spent the whole of that year singing and listening to the old songs.

Just before Christmas 1919, Leo was recalled to India, to Raw-
alpindi, and when Flo and Spike rejoined him in the New Year
it was to live in Kirkee at 5, Climo Road, where the head of the
house was now a newly promoted Quarter-Master Sergeant.
Spike genuinely believes that he actually began to take notice of
the world about then. He would not see it in the future through
what he calls the servile eyes of his father. Harry Secombe remembered how in the war he and Spike:

> . . . used to talk a lot about India, but there was a lot of conflict
> there. He wasn't allowed to play with the officers' children –
> all that sort of stuff. And all that being taught to clap your
> hands for a servant to come – well, if you did that sort of thing
> at Catford . . . you'd get a clip round the ear-hole.[3]

Spike never wanted to play with any but the progeny of other ranks. His dislike of the typical Indian officer was realized in *The Goon Show*. The characters all represented real people in life, like the perverse Colonel Bludnok:

> *He was based on all these Indian colonels I've seen who are all corrupt and screwing fellow officers' wives. Selling the regimental silver all the time, and knocking off Indian women in their tents when they were on manoeuvres. Did I know that when I was a kid? Yes, I remember very clearly.*

Apart from two Anglo-Indian boys, he enjoyed himself best with native children. I have the feeling that Spike's early childhood in India left a great deal to be desired. When his father was not with Flo on the stage, he was frequently away on tours of duty. It would seem that Leo was his soul-mate. Besides which Spike was one of a few boys in a girls' school.

He has an incredible knack of keeping in touch with the past, and an eerie sense of anticipating questions. Like 'just today' he was speaking to Marie Lenihan who used to take him to school in Poona – she's seventy-six now. Marie Kathleen Lenihan – he's not sure but he thinks she's Irish. Her mind is marvellously clear and she was saying how he looked very Irish when he was young. And he has a letter 'from her here' and she says:

> *I asked the nuns and one and all they would chuck you under the chin and say, 'He has the face of an angel.' You had very dark hair, long eyelashes and true Irish blue eyes. You were so quiet except when you were aroused. . . .*

But not all the nuns were the same. The Mother Superior was, in Spike's words, 'a proper cow!' He'd have 'thrown her into a pit full of hissing snakes and just left her there for a while'. She 'bawled' him out in front of the whole school because he fell in a pool of mud in the school ground. And he was 'covered in this mud and so embarrassed' that he got out of the school and 'got a tonga home'.

And it's on such occasions that we learn a little about relationships between Spike and his mother. Flo thought that the whole thing was a storm in a tea-cup and failed to see that her son had been held up to bullying ridicule. Whatever she believed Spike has never forgotten her inaction:

> *My mother thought nothing of it; said, 'Don't worry, just go*

back to school tomorrow.' I didn't return the rest of the day and, on the following morning, this nun stood me up in front of the whole school of girls and screamed and shouted at me. It was then that I realized there are monsters in skirts among the Catholic faithful. I've never gotten over it to this very day – screaming and shouting at me. The cow! I could have become an atheist – or a Protestant.

And then, as 'if recollection can only bear so much pain, he remembers that Mother Fabian was beautiful. She was lovely. She used to get flushed in the face when she was angry. . . . But he seems to be hiding something . . . something about Flo . . . it's as if he wants her to be like Mother Fabian . . . there's an unease between him and his mother . . . he does that all the time . . . he interposes ideas and hides behind words . . . Much of Spike Milligan's life is remembrance and his memory is peopled by ghosts . . . He thought he became a writer to exorcize the faults in the father he loved:

While Uncle Willie would shout about the Easter Rising, Dad would keep his mouth shut. The Connaught Rangers regiment mutinied in 1920, just down the road from us in Poona, and I never heard of the mutiny. That young man executed by firing-squad and all his comrades sent to prison, and I never knew a bloody thing about it until you mentioned it a few days ago. But he just wanted an easy life . . . an easy life with the army . . . I really believe that my father would never have died had they not taken India away from him.

Spike knew all his father's weaknesses, but he never saw him as a weak man. Indeed, while he spent all his life fighting his mother, he felt that he had to prove himself to Leo:

I wrote Puckoon *to prove that I was Irish and to prove to my father that I was a writer . . . that was a great pride to me – that I was actually an author. It was an Irish book, and I thought: Can I write without ever having been there? Do the Irish carry the literary seeds of their race in their stories, in their father's stories? When it was published, everybody thought I'd been to Ireland. . . .*

But he hadn't. Not even once in all Leo's furloughs had Spike ever been taken to Ireland. When his father applied for 'home' leave he meant London, and nowhere else. But Leo was in the original cleft stick: he was a member of an army that was at war with his own countrymen. Maybe, however, by the time the Black n' Tans were at work in Ireland, Spike's father was beginning to let his Irish blood simmer a little, because, for the first time as a soldier of the crown, Leo Milligan expressed a political opinion: '"See that blackguard, Cromwell, and that Protestant bastard, King Billy?" And,' says Spike, 'he never knew either of them.'

The ensuing political and geographical *débâcle* is captured brilliantly in *Puckoon*, which mythical village is a goonlike microcosm of complicated Ireland. In the novel the author continues to confuse, quite consciously, quite deliberately, truth with fiction, fancy with fact. At times the British Army metamorphoses into the IRA, which, when we consider General Tom Barry's life as a republican guerilla commander, having previously served on the Somme, is as likely as any other Irish reality, and certainly mirrored in the serious side of Uncle Willie.

Spike says that much of *Puckoon*'s world is, in the remark of Captain Boyle of *Juno and the Paycock*, 'in a state of chassis':

> *That's how* Puckoon *is. All the time nobody agreeing with anybody else. Father Rudden, you know, was half Red Indian. He baptized me. It's a wonder he didn't tomahawk me in the holy water font. Yes, the British Army in* Puckoon *does become the IRA and vice versa. They are interchangeable. But they were supporting Ulster, you see – they had British troops there backing up Carson. Today the Protestants are firing on the British Army and the IRA. And even old Grandfather Kettleband is round* Puckoon *somewhere, lying to attention in bed. Everything with him is so military.*

When, as a child, he was lonely, he would make up friends to keep him company. Nowadays he speaks about the characters of his books as if they are quite real:

> Puckoon *could have been exploited much more . . . he could have warned the other people in the book that they were being written as they went along . . . and they would have had him committed to a mental asylum because they thought he was mad . . . then he would convince the psychiatrist that 'he' was being written as he went along . . . they're all trapped inside*

this goldfish bowl of a book . . . they don't know that there's another world . . . they're completely in my power – victims of me – but they don't know it. They're being born as I write . . . The Milligan is the only one who had any idea about what was going on – he was waiting to get into the book. He was pre the author . . . what you might call the original preconception . . . I could have exploited the idea no end . . . had them pleading with me to release them into another book, like, say, War and Peace.

Knowing that the fictional *Puckoon* is almost more autobiographical than many of his memoirs, I pressed him about the plans he had envisaged for the crazy characters and eventually he admitted that indeed he had written more:

Yes, you're right; it was a much longer work . . . but parts of it were too sad, so I asked my father to burn them, which he did, very reluctantly, in Woy Woy. I wish I'd listened to him now. . . . I must be the first one who ever wrote a book in which the author spoke to his characters. . . . In parts of the book I had The Milligan warning people about the author . . . but of course I have the last word. . . . I'm so all-powerful that I just put him into the lunatic asylum where, while still under tranquillization, he constantly mutters, 'You bastard, Milligan, I'll get you for this. . . . He kept threatening the author but as soon as he started to make it a struggle, I put him away . . . that's how governments make restrictive laws too, isn't it?

Was The Milligan the 1916 revolutionary Spike wanted his father to be?

Oh yes. It all had to do with the terrible power that Britain had in Ireland or India at the beginning of the century. . . .

The real Leo Milligan is joined in the book by the real Father Rudden of Poona days who is resurrected to play the part of The Milligan's chaplain, confessor, Godcatcher, and 'patronizer':

'What's going on here?' said Father Rudden, issuing from his vestry, his face covered in shaving soap. 'What are you doing in me churchyard?' he roared, pulling off a layer of policemen.
'This man is a member of the IRA,' they said, pointing at The Milligan.
'Nonsense, this man is my gardener.'

'Then your gardener is a member of the IRA,' they said,
dragging The Milligan away.

'Stop!' said the priest *'Gentlemen,'* he said in tones most
contrite, but continuing to shave, *'if you'll step into the vestry,
I will admit the entire plot to capture the Queen.'*[4]

Spike mourns the lost chapters of *Puckoon* and is convinced
that it would have been an even better book with all its parts
intact:

> Such a lot more was in the book as well, but I burned it. What
> a pity. It's a very strange, destructive thing . . . like a painter
> burning his own paintings. . . . Van Gogh did a lot of that, you
> know. It's a sort of pyromanic, pyrrhic victory against yourself.
> The ultimate masochism, 'Look what I'm doing! I'm actually
> burning myself!'

How Spike ever learned his Irish history is difficult to say. He
thinks himself that his father used to tell stories about Uncle
Willie, some of which should have been attributed to Leo himself.

Things for the Milligans became much easier when Spike's
father was promoted Quarter-Master Sergeant:

> Beer was cheap but now he found that he could get champagne
> for nothing, which was even cheaper, so my parents began to
> get used to the good life.

Material perks apart, life for Leo as a Quarter-Master Sergeant
must have been good because the officers delegated so much
responsibility. Since most troop-training was left to the NCOs,
it is not surprising that a sleeve of stripes was frequently more
feared than an epaulette of pips.

After the war in Europe the character of the British Army was
never the same. To men who had literally mucked with their
principals in trenches from Baghdad to Berlin, the 'officer class'
was a mystery no longer:

> The war had changed many things. Not the least of the changes
> was a slackening in the hitherto sacred military principle that
> a shining belt buckle meant that the wearer was a good soldier.
> But in that relaxation, it would seem, contact was lost with the
> rank and file.[5]

Hard on the release of the jailed Connaught Rangers, early in 1922, came the news that the following Irish regiments of the British Army were to be disbanded: The Royal Irish Regiment, The Royal Irish Fusiliers, The Leinster Regiment, The Royal Munster Fusiliers, The Royal Dublin Fusiliers and the Connaught Rangers.

In tears at Windsor Castle on 12th June, 1922, King George V said:

> . . . *I pledge my word that within these ancient and historic walls your colours will be treasured, honoured and protected as hallowed memorials of the glorious deeds of brave and loyal regiments.*

No wonder Spike stuck with the Royal Artillery when he joined up. There was only one *Irish* regiment left: The Royal Enniskillens had been saved from dissolution by the pleas of the Orange Lodges, and a Milligan could hardly have thrown in his lot with them.

Six India! India!

They belonged to Bengal and to Burma,
to Madras and to the Punjab, but they were all my
people.

Sara Jeannette Duncan, *A Mother in India*

> *As a boy*
> *I watched India through fresh*
> *Empirical eyes.*
> *Inside my young khaki head*
> *I grew, not knowing any other world.*
> *My father was a great warrior,*
> *My mother was beautiful*
> *and never washed dishes,*
> *other people did that,*
> *I was only four, I remember*
> *they cleaned my shoes,*
> *made my bed . . .*[1]

We talked, me and Spike, about the difficulty of making sense from the recent past; it hadn't as yet, it seemed, become history. Spike can recall 1922, when he was four years of age, with fearful acuity. What Poona was like, how his mother behaved towards him – smothering him with love one moment, and going into uncontrollable rages and beating him the next. And his parents treated the servants differently; Leo was kind:

> *but, once again, the natives were the Irish of India. They were*
> *the step lower. He was kind to them whereas my mother would*
> *hit them!*

But more cruel yet was Flo's father, Grandfather Kettleband:

> *He hated the servants. Hated everybody. He'd hit the groom*
> *and stroke the dog. Used to get up in the morning and say in*
> *the voice of military command: 'Tea in pot! Dog off chain!'*
> *And my dad always mimicked him: 'Newspaper in! Dog out!'*

Young Milligan's formative years were more sheltered than secure. At his Raj school for girls he was happy but lonely, and was learning to be superior to the natives with whom he felt an affinity. His father was 'a warrior', but the uniform hid much that only the eyes of one small boy could see. Leo was a very smart soldier but servile. Spike is ruthless in his cruelly objective detailed examination of the character of the man he loved best of all:

> Being an Irishman, he always thought that he had to mind his place – and all the people who talked 'Laike thett, you know' to whom he felt inferior. He could have been an officer from the beginning, but he didn't think he had the wherewithal; yet he took honours in mathematics in the Services Exams. But he always thought that, because he was Irish – well, of course we were taught to be subservient. You were a man of the line! English could be sahibs but we were the soldiers.

They sang words to the bugle-call melody:

> Officers' wives get pudding
> and pies
> But we poor boys get
> skilly.

In the parasitical world of Empire, of great, little and lesser fleas, Milligan felt that his people were the ad infinitum.

> When you wet the bed first it is warm, then it gets cold. His mother put on the oilsheet. That had the queer smell. His mother had a nicer smell than his father . . .[2]

Like the boy in *Portrait of the Artist as a Young Man*, Spike wet the bed and, even now, wonders why. The psychologists should have taken a look at Flo, a craw-thumping Catholic who, throughout his life, has weighed her son down with holy medals and rosary beads and original sin.

> Oh yes, my mother's religion was dreadfully bitter. Of course then she was English and you know they were never cut out to be Catholics. They have such a severe God, you know. She did to her son what she couldn't do to her Catholic husband who was less than devout and with whom she was deeply in love.

Leo was neither an atheistic Catholic nor a Catholic atheist. He was deeply anti-clerical and deeply religious. On Sundays Leo used to ask about Holy Communion: 'And what wines are being served? Is there a better vintage at the second Mass than at the first? . . . Ah yes, there's a nice little Beaujolais at six o'clock but you'll get a better one at eleven.'

> *My father had to leave church in Poona one Sunday. There was this Madrasi priest saying the Mass. In Madrasi it sounded to Dad like, 'Silly bugger, silly bugger, you're a lot of silly buggers.' And this 'silly bugger' thing went on for so long that my father, who had a sense of humour like nobody's, crawled out of the chapel in hysterics. He used to make me laugh. He was so irreligious.*

And yet Spike swears he wouldn't have been without his Catholicism, much as it screwed him up, and 'got things wrong' for him. No, he wouldn't have been without it. When anybody asks to which religion he owes allegiance, Milligan immediately asserts:

> *'I'm a Catholic!' and then they say, 'Well you don't go to church and that?' and I say, 'No, I don't,' and they say, 'How can you be a Catholic if you don't go to church?' But I just am a Catholic. I was brought up one.*

Such an upbringing does not, however, mean that even church rite is beyond his sense of the ridiculous. Nothing is sacrosanct. Anything but. 'The Credo' from *The Bed-Sittingroom* echoes parts of the Mass: 'The Absolution', 'The Kyrie Eleison' and 'The Gloria':

> PLASTIC MAN: Save me, merciful Lord, from the terrible temptations and perversions of the rubber . . .
>
> SEAMAN: Oh Lord . . . give me higher wages and a shorter working week . . .
>
> MATE: God, save me and I'll give up being an atheist . . . Goddy . . . .
>
> CAPTAIN: Oh Lord . . . merciful Lord . . . how shall I reside in Thy kingdom?
>
> FORTNUM: By paying a purely nominal rent of fifty guineas a week.
>
> MATE: I'll pay it . . . I'll pay it . . .[3]

After which God is unmasked by Kak, and Captain calls Kak a blasphemer. This device would appear to be Milligan praying behind his mind, telling God that he's only joking. Spike remembers his religious duties ... remembers the Litany, the Office, the Latin. ... And when they ended the Tridentine Mass he was upset:

> *Why try to mend something that's not broken? Make the Mass ordinary; like a Protestant service? I suppose, if we think of the fixed order, the established sequence of the Mass, I must mean extraordinary.*

He doesn't want a religion made easy, because he can't have complete faith in a belief he fully comprehends:

> *They took away the mystery. And the Pope thinks he has upgraded it, you know – plastic chalice and vegetable host. No more Corpus Christi. None of that cannibal stuff. Did you hear about the Irish vegetarian who only eats animals that eat grass?*

He liked the smell of his mother. When she would dress in her finery to go to the theatre, appear on the stage, or spend a day at the races. For all their wilful battles of personality he loved her dearly, if at times a little apprehensively. Maybe if she had changed the wet sheet herself and not left the job to the ayah. ...

> *She could be coldly brutal to me. Beat me round the ears and still love me. Brutal without being cruel – she could make a distinction. Her tempers terrified me because she'd fly right off the handle for no apparent reason, or at the slightest provocation.*

5, Climo Road must have been like a shrine, with its candles, crucifixes and Christian creed, and the most oppressive thing to the barely committed is the endless kneeling each night to say endless decades of the Rosary; caustic Catholics talk of 'kneeling your way to Heaven'.

But, before the prayers, the evenings were good fun; Leo and his wife and sister-in-law, Eileen, would sing while Flo played the piano and Hughie Kettleband joined in on the banjo and ukulele. Grandmother Kettleband sewed the stage costumes and murmured the words of the songs while her husband growled intolerantly at the ayah who obviously was not showing proper servility while bathing his grandson for bed.

Spike liked the singing; he liked his Uncle Hughie: he was fascinated by Hughie's instruments. But, young as he was, he knew how to feel shame that this world of the Raj was made of servants and masters. Nothing in life abuses dignity more than the very sight of somebody doing something for somebody that somebody is well able to do for himself. One can sense that Spike is of such a mind in his sardonic use of the Urdu phrase: *Ither ow, Kom Kurrow* ('Come here! Do your work!'). He ends his poem 'India! India!':

> Ither ow
> Kom Kurrow
> *Yet, in time I found them gentler*
> *than the khaki people.*
> *They smiled in their poverty*
> *After dark, when the khaki people*
> *were drunk in the mess*
> *I could hear Minema and*
> *her family praying in their godown.*
> *In the bazaar the khaki men*
> *are brawling.*
> *No wonder they asked us to leave.*[4]

Milligan shakes his head in disbelief and says:

> *No wonder they asked us to leave?*

'Us' and 'them'. And Spike never considered himself to be part of anything. Even his own mind was 'inside my young khaki head'.

The Convent of Jesus and Mary, Poona, was a strange school for any mother to choose for her son, but then the young Flo was a strange woman. Spike thinks that she was trying to protect him 'from the realities of life'. It doesn't seem to have occurred to her that a boy might feel out of place at an all-girls' school conducted by women. Even the most liberated, the most equal of girls seldom have the same interests, share the same needs, or play at the same games as boys. Spike was one of only half a dozen other boys attending the Convent School, but he says he didn't mind the preponderance of girls. He didn't even object when his school report card referred to him as 'Miss' Milligan.

To disregard the upbringing of their sons is a common fault among Irish fathers, although it is also true to say that they seldom pack them off to public school, a fate once feared by the children of English expatriates throughout the Empire. Milligan says:

> Nobody ever liked the Raj, but when you saw the children, their children, rejected in English boarding schools and more out of place every time they returned to India, you couldn't but feel sorry for them. But that, for the most part, was the way their fathers and mothers had been reared – orphans with parents who didn't care.

Spike, a desperately lonely child, always needing the encouragement of his father, would have cut a pathetic picture at school in England at a time when officers' children were fortunate to get back to their families in India once a year. Had he come to England out of term, he would have been welcomed by his aunt Kathleen in Sittingbourne, though his grandfather William, in Poplar, seems to have wanted nothing better from his family than to be left severely alone. Otherwise, all the Milligans were in Poona or Ireland.

Flo, a woman of quite independent outlook – a twentieth-century lady who would have loved to have been able to pursue a full-time career in show-business, seems to have found children tiresome and their rearing time-consuming. Leo did as much as he could, but he had a full-time job trying to outwit the army brass and support a wife and family.

There is no resentment in Spike towards the parents who must bear some responsibility for his unsettled childhood. Milligan believes that he did rather well, and would indeed have done better had it not been for the exigent needs of his father's job. Leo was often away for months on end and new postings frequently meant a change of school for the young Terence Alan:

> When I was a boy and at one school in India, I came first – top of the class! Three times running! Then this moving started – going from one school to another, and yet another. And in the end all the school systems were different. I sort of got lost and turned in on myself – into a world of fantasy.

Since then, he says, 'I've become scholastic and I read and read. My house is always full of books. The rooms are full of the bloody things.' He even carried them in his knapsack during the war. At bombed-out places, if he saw some good books he'd 'knock them off and bring them home on leave'. That, he will boast, is how he started his library.

Spike Milligan's modesty in claiming to have been among the most ill-r̲ ̲d children of his day is probably his most arrogant boast. It is as if, like Shostakovitch, he wants it to be believed that he alone is responsible for his learning. And so he will tell you in apparent humility that at home in Climo Road there was plenty of sheet music, but only two novels, *Robinson Crusoe* and *The Swiss Family Robinson*.

Maybe it is to Dr Wyss's genteel household that he owes his pathological hatred of moral turpitude, for Spike has a robust tongue and a clean mind. Milligan in conversation has an army vocabulary that leaves little to the imagination. His words can be rudely descriptive and blasphemous by turn, but never less than meaningful. Indeed, frequently the surrogate adjective lends a powerfully emphatic elegance to a language that owes nothing to the vulgarity of those who employ a double-entendre in writing and speech:

> *There was this fella, you see, caught with a girl in a doorway in my father's native town in Ireland. Brought up to court and the judge looks at him and says, 'Yer a dirty scoundrel and I'm goin' to give yeh six months.' And as yer man is goin' down the dock he screams back at the judge, 'Six minits or six months! yeh won't stop people fuckin' in Sligo!'*

Spike is fond of claiming that 'the old stories are best'. Many of Leo's 'jokes' find their way into Milligan's work, so that in *The Looney*, Magistrate Mrs Thelma Skugs gives a man three months 'for screwing in a doorway':

> *'There's far too much of this going on,' she had chastised him. He was dragged from the dock shouting, 'You'll never stop fucking in Kilburn.'*[5]

Introversion, then, may have been fed, on the other hand, by the work of the secretive Defoe, with his world of seeming reality, peopled with solitary figures from Moll Flanders to Colonel Jack, to Crusoe himself, maybe responsible to some extent for the some-times loneliness of the gregarious Milligan:

> *I always think of other people as necessary. That's about the*

way I think of other people. It's because of the nature of writing as an occupation – its loneliness; a form of self-imprisonment.

Leo's great attraction was his spontaneous wit and his easy charm. Spike counted the hours he was away and the minutes to his return. At times his father had all the white arrogance of Defoe, and at other times the Protestant gentility of Jan Wyss. This is not surprising since both *Robinson Crusoe* and *The Swiss Family Robinson* are, by admission of Wyss's editor, the same work. When I told Spike that Daniel Defoe was a fervent follower of King William of Orange and Jan Wyss was a bitter anti-Catholic, he remarked:

Is that so? Well, all I can say is, it's lucky for them that my old man never knew this or he would have cheerfully dug them up and kicked fuck out of them.

During the early twenties the security of army life came under threat and, although Leo was not aware of it at the time, his main hope for staying on in the army was a continuation of the Irish 'troubles' which Lloyd George was trying desperately to resolve.

Leo worried that every unemployed person signing the register in Britain meant a threat to every soldier in India. Besides which, the government was threatening a ten per cent cut in overall public spending:

'We'll be the first to go,' he told his wife. 'That's parliament all over: no love for the army except when they need us!'

In Ireland the President of the Republic, Eamon de Valera, received a letter from the Prime Minister proposing a peace conference. Within a fortnight, General Nevil MacReady, C. in C. British Forces, and de Valera agreed that a general truce should come into effect at noon on 11th July, 1921.

Lloyd George was cockahoop and the war-mongering sections of the Tory party dismayed. Now Leo Milligan's job was really in jeopardy; talk of defence cut-backs and of running down the army were rife, and the lotus-eaters of the imperial world began to think of home again, and worry that they might be joining the same soup queues as everybody else.

But God, they say, seldom closes one door without opening another. Winston Churchill said that the Russians were trying to encourage disaffection among the tribesmen of Afghanistan.

Leo prayed, 'Send us, O Lord, war in our time,' and, by the mercy of God, his prayers were answered. Almost overnight there were fifty-thousand troops manning the Afghan heights. Another theatre of war for Colonel Blimp meant another job-saving tour of duty for Leo Milligan.

Better still, there was more than enough conflict going around to keep the troops occupied in the chief cities and towns of India. Bombay, Calcutta and Poona saw Mahatma Gandhi praying his way through India like a biblical blitzkrieg. Pacifists became terrified of 'preachers' and 'peace', for the 'holy men' had made them synonymous with vengeance. And Leo's workforce put in hours of overtime exacting bitter revenge.

Throughout 1921 the British kept their hands off Gandhi while arresting practically every other Congress leader. Then on 10th March, 1922 they took him into custody and sentenced him to six years:

> *The crucial fact was, however, that there was not a ripple of protest anywhere in India as Gandhi went to jail.*[6]

It was on that day, just weeks before his fourth birthday, that Spike Milligan saw 'A harmless frail man with no weapons' being taken off to Yeravada prison. He never forgot his father's words dismissing Gandhi as:

> *A trouble-maker, son, that's all.*

Many years later, Spike wrote:

> *I once, as a child,*
> *saw Mahatma Gandhi*
> *Walk past the old Sappers Lines,*
> *Climo Road.*
> *He was on his way to Yerod Gaol.*
> *'He's not as black as he's painted,'*
> *said my kind grandmother,*
> *But I found out he was not painted,*
> *It was his real colour.*[7]

Seven Finger Painting

To my own Gods I go
It may be that they shall give me greater ease
Than your cold Christ and tangled trinities.

Rudyard Kipling, 'Lispeth'

Spike as a boy was innocent, shy and introspective – 'solitary' he said. And, sacred cows apart, India was hardly a sanctuary for animals: peasants are not made in the image of Francis of Assisi. Which is not to say that cruelty and indifference to the suffering of animals were the prerogative of the Indian. As Pauline Scudamore recounts, Spike watched in horror as British troops diverted themselves by trying to drown a monkey. Failing that they beat it to death with sticks.

> *I think it was then that I knew how sadistic men could be. It was the whole idea of doing such a terrible thing for sheer enjoyment. And, mark you, people do it because they actually get a kick out of it. They say that the man, Ryan, who shot all the people in Hungerford did so because he was mad – I don't know, what if he just enjoyed killing just for the hell of it?*

Because of the danger of rabies, stray animals, to be controlled by dog-handlers, were often shot on sight and, on one occasion, Spike had to ask that a maimed animal be put out of its misery. Another time a servant accidently rammed a stick down the stomach of the Milligans' pet duck. Before that, his dog, Boxer, disappeared without trace. And then Spike wasn't allowed pets at all.

The loss of Boxer affected Spike so deeply that he tried to write the incident out of his memory:

> *They never told me*
> *when you died*
> *to spare me pain*
> *in case I cried.*
> *So then to*
> *those adult fears*

> *denied you then*
> *my childhood tears.*[1]

Spike loves nature and believes she is in need of protection, but he doesn't confuse people with pets. He knows which from what. He loves flowers and children but, like Shaw, he wouldn't cut their heads off and stick them in pots. Life with Milligan is a personal battle, whether it has to do with child abuse or the environment. He believes that sins against humanity do not deserve absolution.

Apart from the admonition to judge not lest he himself be judged, I doubt very much, when the time came, that Spike would be prepared to compound one wrong by committing another. I don't see Milligan in the hanging lobby.

Maybe there is something recondite, little known to him, about his retrospective anger: a recollection of the Poona dog-controller firing from such a close range that he blew the dog's spine in half and, while it still wagged its tail, another shot made its eyes pop out.

Prisoners of the past need Madeleine cakes if only to test the memory. Deprived children of deprived childhoods invariably survive; those deprived of childhood come to manhood filled with inhibitions and guilt. Borstal boys, like Albert Camus or Frank Norman, grew up to be as confused as any other public schoolboy: terrified at the immensity of the human dilemma – the size of life. And the poets and painters who, with Picasso, 'took a lifetime to learn how to paint like an infant', or Byron, about whom Goethe said he was only great as a poet, 'as soon as he reflects, he is a child', must have missed out on something at the beginning. Certainly Milligan knows this feeling.

A simple adventure like Cowboys and Indians must have been a funny game played by a white boy and some child natives of Poona but, because Hollywood is universal, the same Tom Mixs, Ken Maynards, Buck Joneses and Hopalong Cassidys shot the same redskins and badmen from Melbourne to Minnesota, from Bombay to Birmingham. The same kids have always refused to play dead in any colour, in any country in the world, much to our chagrined annoyance.

And yet Spike must have been more confused than most of his play-group. Speaking of his father, he says:

You know he used to dress up in full Hollywood Western gear

*in Poona, and have his picture taken. Then he'd send it to me,
signed: 'Happy Christmas, Dad'! For years I grew up in the
belief that Santa Claus was a fucking cowboy.*

Such innocence, and yet, when you're as lonely as Spike, your
life must seem as solitary as that of the young George Washington – so isolated that he never learned how to lie. Milligan
was expected to ignore the civilization in which he was growing,
and complained that he wasn't allowed to absorb Indian or Burmese culture. It would, he thought, in a way have made up for
the white man's burden which every Anglo-Indian child was
forced to bear whenever the real coolie felt mutinous.

The Indians had wonderful songs and music and architecture,
but the child of the Raj was always pressed into a sort of acceptance that things non-British had no worth. Nothing of value
was supposed to come out of India, and Spike complained that
although he spoke fluent Urdu when he was thirteen, nobody
encouraged him to persevere:

*Why didn't they try and keep that alive in me at least? I'd
have had a second language then, wouldn't I? It was just never
valued as being anything that could possibly be worth learning
or preserving.*

Because Milligan came across the world late in life it is surprising that his sincerity has not got him into more trouble. He loves
life and the earth and everything in it. He's an environmentalist,
convinced that if we don't look after the world people will either
blow it to bits or let it leak away through holes in the ozone
layer.

*The universe doesn't belong to us and we have no right to
vandalize it. After all we are only caretakers like any other
generation.*

To him there is no mystery – enigma simply needs explanation:
mankind may have been around for millions of years but, to
Spike, it is a fairly young family. If age was as old as historians
would have Milligan believe, why, he will argue, are children still
treated so badly? Why is civilization such a long time coming?

There's a fearful honesty about Milligan. Some of his admissions are such that you want to protect him from the wide world.
Oh, he's sophisticated all right, make no mistake about that, but

it is a sophistication redolent of a more civilized society than the one into which he was thrust. His truth has a fragrance such as has not lingered around the adult world for a long time.

That grown-ups tell lies is a lesson children learn the hard way. So Spike hid himself in art, for artists seldom grow up and are always truthful. Before he could ever tell the difference between the two, Milligan wanted life to be like art. But then, too, Spike tends to imagine that humanity is a religion, that everybody has a soul. You feel that a year or two in a tenement wouldn't have done his childhood a great deal of harm. He might have become a little 'street-wise'.

He recalls how one particular Indian kid could outrun him, and it worried Spike that it made him angry when that same kid had the arrogance of competitiveness. As an 'inferior' the boy should have lost, and other members of the master race would have thrashed the child for his impertinence, but Milligan couldn't have cared less about being beaten by a real Indian or an Anglo-Indian; what really annoyed Spike was that he had been beaten.

> I'm terribly competitive, you know. Always was – at whatever game, cricket, rugby . . . Not so much in rugby, I think, because, although I was fairly good on the wing – speedy, you know – if any of the opposing backs were fast enough to come to me I'd give them the ball: 'Here, is this what you're looking for?' And I'd hand it to them. Otherwise I hated being a good loser. I'll never forget that kid as long as I live. His people were so poor that he didn't have any clothes.

And yet I can see Spike's conqueror more clearly than any of the ones who vanquished my childhood. It is because Milligan's descriptiveness is so graphic. I can see the legs of that kid running Spike into the ground and I can see Milligan's long limbs doing their damndest to stave off defeat. I hear his commentary, but see the race. We know then why, when Redon and Gauguin got close to the Symbolists in French poetry and became interested in the power of suggestion and inference, they felt that the artist must 'clothe the idea in visible form'.

Milligan, agonizing for articulation, eager to express himself, found as he developed that, for him, words proved to be the better paint; paper the more welcoming canvas. He had been to the music-hall and the palace of varieties – his parents worked in them. He had been to the dance-halls – he made music in them. So if the tortured Toulouse-Lautrec saw the Moulin Rouge as a 'joyless place where people seek to escape', Milligan could see it that way too. He could also see it through the happy eyes of Renoir and that is Spike's salvation.

Why the earlier preoccupation with the sketch-pad? Was it the lack of literature? Were pictures the surrogate books? Was sketching a second prize? Spike is, what they call in Ireland, 'a great man for the drawing'. That is why the legs of the Milligan take over in *Puckoon* and why Grandfather Kettleband lies 'to attention even in bed'. *The Goon Show* scripts are made up in the same word-pictures, as if they are translated from a series of pictorial images. Joyce had a phrase for it, 'The ineluctable modality of the visible: at least that if no more, thought through my eyes.' In *The Little Pot Boiler*, for example, an infantry unit under attack on p. 42 are looking across to a blank p. 43 and an officer pointing says:

That page looks quieter![2]

It is not surprising that works of twentieth-century literature did not find their way into the Milligan household – he was, at that time, outside the Catholic pale. It is most odd, however, that Defoe and Wyss were so popular with the Milligans. Catholic life revolves round Fridays, that hour of good intentions. Robinson Crusoe named Man-Friday because Defoe knew the importance of the day in the Catholic ritual.

Fridays have a special significance for members of the Holy Roman Catholic and Apostolic Church – a sort of religious exacerbation. Pain and ecstacy. The weekly reminder of the crucifixion – the Fifth Day Seventh Day Adventists with no need to be convinced of the second coming – Christ is always there behind that tabernacle door. There are at least fifty-two Fridays, no less than twelve first Fridays, and there is Holy Friday, Golden Friday and the big one, Good Friday, in every year.

Spike's Friday was of pisces blest. He seemed always to be getting ready for Sunday. Grandfather Kettleband would get his suit out and have it all ironed up by the ayah, out of whom, given the chance, he would have soundly beaten the heresy. And all the servants knew that the Milligans didn't eat meat on Friday. They went about saying, 'Today we don't eat meat.' Went around giving all sorts of reasons why Catholics didn't eat meat just on that one day.

Somebody might knock on the door selling newspapers, and the
servants would say, for small talk, 'Oh, by the way, this is
Friday, we're not eating meat.'

Catholics in Ireland seldom question their religion until they have given it up. The mysteries of the Church must be accepted without challenge. Why are there three divine persons in one? There just are. How did Jesus come back from the dead? He just did. And that, in Ireland, is 'normal'.

But what about growing up in India? To garb a child in such an immutable faith and expect him to grow among the heretics is not only bad-mannered, it's cruel to the child.

Much worse, however, is to treat a boy who has been born with an innate respect for the word to one of the most racist novels ever to vandalize a nursery library. Why did Leo buy such a book as *Robinson Crusoe* for his house? Spike says:

He just didn't know. He was so ignorant, you see.

And yet, if Christianity was a problem for Christians, religion didn't make life any easier for the people of the sub-continent. In 1923 Pandhit Nehru was complaining that 'Conditions in India have never been worse. . . . The only education the masses are getting is in communal hatred.' And still the Milligans were blissfully unaware of the powder-keg of non-violence.

While Leo was away on tours of duty, Flo was concerned to look her best in the heat of Poona. And why? According to Milligan, the Maharajah of Agacote fancied his mother. He used to lend Flo his carriage – at the beginning to go and see Leo when he was in hospital. Spike says that it was sheer madness. There was, he says, 'this ordinary military hospital with ordinary motor cars pulling up, and here's this four in hand with gold things on the front and two flunkeys on the back, and a sergeant's daughter gets out! To visit her sergeant husband!'

Then Leo and Flo got the use of the carriage to do the social rounds. Maybe to Poona racecourses. They could ride in state:

. . . and there would be this sergeant getting out of this golden
coach. It's like seeing a dustman getting out of the Queen's
carriage at Buckingham Palace.

Incongruous? It was the jazz age and the slump – dancing all night to keep the depression at bay. Talk was that the Labour

Party might come to power in Britain and abolish the army, give the colonies back to the colonials and make John Bull a second-class power. How very like a whale. Flo, it seemed, never realized that the Empire was under threat.

Leo and Flo liked nothing better than to be seen in high society:

> *They used to go to the races and lose, they'd take twenty-five rupees each – I know that's not a lot of money but it was for this particular family.*

His parents must have been living beyond their means for Spike knew that racing was a pastime they could ill afford.

Spike himself did a little gambling in India when he was small. He used to go to the race-track at Poona. It was a few miles away and he used to walk there. His mother would give him two or three annas – about sixpence. Once he backed a horse called 'Kadir Hajaz' which belonged to the Maharajah of Sholapur whose racing colours were orange. The tents were white and the holy colour green and he remembered that Uncle Willie had told him that the Irish tricolour was green, white and orange. The pukka people in the wine tent said 'cheers' after each drink so he also backed another horse owned by the Maharajah called 'Cheer-io'. They both won. They say that a first win usually makes a person a compulsive gambler, but Spike never felt that way, even in Australia.

While his parents were in the royal enclosure, Spike used to go into the centre of the course and bet with the Hindu bookies:

> *. . . all wearing running shoes and as soon as the races were over they'd sprint for cover.*

Eight London Pride

They were marching on Londinium
To put down a revolt
By British yobs
And British slobs
All drunk on hops and malt.

Spike Milligan, *Startling Verse for All the Family*

The first Labour administration had come to power in Britain under Ramsay MacDonald. Having saved the City of London from itself, the Labour administration fell but, in the spring of 1924, the dealers of Throgmorton Street and Wall Street were content that the socialist MacDonald had kept bolshevisim out of Western Europe and extreme Conservatives were relieved that the only thing he nationalized was the national debt.

At thirty-four Leo was promoted to Regimental Sergeant-Major. He was to be allowed to stay on in the Royal Artillery until 1929 and he was posted to Burma. Spike and his mother didn't join Leo for almost a year and they had barely reached Burma when they had to return to Poona because Grandma Kettleband was showing signs of mental instability. She had been declining since her husband's death in 1923. How did he go? Spike remembered:

Aneurysm. He used to blow the bugle and they think that he blew himself to death.

They stayed some months with Grandmother Kettleband, and Spike had to change schools once more.

Flo was pregnant again and it must have been difficult for her to cope with her disturbed mother and a child fretting for his absent father. Maybe too, Spike thinks, in his mother there may have been an element of sexual frustration, what with Leo away and her being a good Catholic. She was, he says, always a very highly strung woman; and that's why she used to beat the servants sometimes, and when they weren't around she'd hit Spike.

She couldn't bear staying in at home when Leo was away at work. She would do local shows on her own or even play the piano in the pit. That would be in either the West End or the Empire cinema in Poona. Sometimes she'd play for the film, sometimes it would be to accompany the acts in what they called cine-variety – where they would screen a film and have a stage show as well. Spike used to sit in the orchestra pit with his mother. But when the film started, his head was always at an angle of ninety degrees trying to watch the screen:

> *No wonder I was always looking up afterwards, like those aviators we used to see in war films.*

In the British General Election of 1924 the Conservatives swept to power in a landslide victory: they got 415 seats against the Labours' 152 and the Liberals' 42. Contrary to what might have been expected, their election didn't leave the expatriates of the Empire any less uneasy about the future.

The India Bill was still waiting in the wings and, to the Raj, it was nothing more than Home Rule by the back door. They had not forgotten 1883 and the then Viceroy, Lord Rippon, a deputy monarch with the language of a republican. The French had given their Indian subjects local government and representation in Parliament. 'Frog wogs' they were called in Pondicherry. But, if you couldn't trust an English Viceroy to do the decent thing, then God bless the memory of the first Empress of India!

The new Prime Minister, Stanley Baldwin, 'the Small-Tonsured One', made at least one unusual Cabinet appointment which should have put most of the British Raj at its ease. When Winston Churchill became Tory Chancellor of the Exchequer everybody knew where he stood on India. Over his dead body would the Empire be broken up.

In the autumn of 1925, after giving Britain and Italy guarantees of peace, Germany came into the League of Nations and signed a non-aggression pact with France and Belgium, never to be broken. And Spike's brother, Desmond Patrick Milligan, was born, in the Military Hospital at Rangoon, on 3rd December, 1925.

The Milligans seem to have lived a fairly nomadic life through the twenties. Leo was frequently away on tours of duty and Flo spent a lot of the time between Poona and Rangoon. It's a tribute to his determined endeavours that Spike, in his final report from the Convent of Jesus and Mary, got an average of 60 marks out of a possible 100. More importantly, in English composition, he netted ninety per cent, with only fourteen per cent for grammar.

When somebody said to him in later life, 'Spike, your syntax and grammar are appalling,' Spike replied that he didn't welcome impediments. Did somebody say that 'punctuation is a matter of opinion'?

In the late summer of 1927, Spike's uncle, Hughie Kettleband, sent word to Flo that their mother had tried to commit suicide. Once again Flo and the two children set off for Poona and once again Spike changed schools.

On the brighter side, Leo's promotion was beginning to mean that he could be more often at home with the family in Rangoon. It meant a lot for Spike to receive letters from his father telling him that when he got back from leave they would all play Cowboys and Indians together, or go hunting and 'Skin the buck'.

He has frequently complained that his boyhood 'always seemed a bit solitary'. He used to think it would be a wonderful thing to have a boy of his own age visit his house and stay for a whole day, 'but somehow it never seemed possible to arrange'. Flo discouraged visits from children.

Milligan thinks his passion for reading derives from this loneliness. He would avidly digest any publication he layed eyes on, no matter where – in bed, over other folks' shoulders, on the floors of lavatories. In later life he was surprised at how little evidence there was of books in the Sellers and Secombe residences.

Spike was disappointed when he received a letter from his father on his eleventh birthday regretting that he could not be with him for the occasion, and then overjoyed when Leo arrived in Poona having wangled a leave. To crown Spike's happiness, his father announced that all arrangements had been made for the whole family to be together in Burma. Spike says that his eleventh birthday was wonderful because he couldn't believe that so many happy things could happen all at once and to the same family.

In January 1929, Spike enrolled at St Paul's Roman Catholic School, Rangoon:

> I went first to the de La Salles, and then to the Jesuits – the Jesuits are the greatest. They're the Christian commandos of religion – they go where nobody has gone before. . . .

And some grammar-conscious nun winced in Poona or heaven. The Jesuits, he thought, 'took up a stance', and he felt sure that most of them would like to see priests able to marry and such. On the whole he sees the Jesuits not as the black-coated brigands castigated by the papacy but as reasonable men.

The author of *Ulysses* would not have appreciated their hypocrisy, but Spike is weighed down by tradition; 'once a Catholic always a Catholic.' And yet, as has been said before, friendship, with Spike, transcends most things, in some cases even morality.

> . . . I have a friend, a Catholic priest, and he had a love affair with this woman . . . nearly destroyed him . . . they had a child that was aborted and it's driven him mad . . . he went away to Sudan or somewhere to get away from it all . . . He's a lovely man. He's completely holy though he drinks like a fish and swears like fuck. But, when I say to him, 'Father, would you bless me?' and he puts his hand to my head, he suddenly turns into a holy man. Just in one second.

Rangoon was good for Spike at the age of twelve. He had a brother of five whom he adored, and his father had company in the evenings.

One visitor, who travelled by bus and called his father 'Milli', used to arrive armed with sheafs of paper – 'A big book of papers,' Spike recalled. He was known as Eric, or Sergeant Blair, and was for ever questioning 'Milli' about things like the roads, upon which Leo was something of an authority. It seemed that George Orwell was doing research for his *Burmese Days*:

> I remember that he was called Sergeant Blair. I remember that he was very thin. I was very thin too and I was glad that somebody else was thin.

Orwell and Leo used to sit outside the Brigade house in Rangoon. They wore shorts and short sleeves. Spike remembered that the author of *1984* had navy blue epaulettes on his jacket which was a shirt, and a navy blue band round his peaked cap. He had three stripes and he used to drink shandy; apart from champagne, which he adored, Spike's father wasn't a great drinker and he used to drink shandy as well.

Orwell made little impression on the young Milligan. Spike never thought much about him although he visited the Milligans quite regularly – once a week, mostly at the weekends and in the evenings. When Spike met him, Leo said, 'Sergeant, this is my son, Terence,' and Spike shook hands with him. But Milligan doesn't remember anything Sergeant Blair ever said:

> *But then Dad was a great conversationalist – the hit of the party, you know.*

It is remarkable that Spike should be able to remember how Orwell's bush jacket would have differed from his father's – the navy blue trimmings indicated that Sergeant Blair was then serving in the Indian Imperial police. And how he evokes the Anglo-Indian idiom with just the simple remembrance that Blair called his father 'Milli' – Orwell was born in Bengal.

> *It was his skinny legs that I couldn't get over. Skinny legs and sloping shoulders. Black hair, I think – or have I seen a photograph of him? Really, I can't remember. I know I didn't get any money from him – ever. And that's strange because visitors – European visitors – always gave kids a few pence. I remember thinking that he called Dad a funny name: I knew a girl called Millie.*

It might have been interesting to know if Leo behaved in a servile manner to a person so conscious of class as Orwell, whom he outranked. Richard Hoggart says that Sergeant Blair called himself a member of the lower-upper middle classes:

> *His point was that his father was a public servant, not a land-owner or a big businessman; so though he had the rank, status and tastes of a gentleman, his salary was modest. He was, in fact, a minor official in the Indian Customs Service. . . .*[1]

In 1927, Leo's father, William Patrick, died in England and four years later Leo Milligan was granted long home leave. Spike, Desmond and Flo preceded him via Calcutta to spend a while with the Kettlebands of Poona. Leo and Flo and the two children sailed from Bombay and arrived at Tilbury on 27th March, 1931.

The National Government of Conservatives, Liberals and Labour, under the premiership of Ramsay MacDonald, was in office. Churchill had resigned the year before when Baldwin accepted the plan for Indian self-government.

Spike was looking forward to coming 'home' to 'a land of chocolate and ice cream'. The England to which he returned was one of fog, smog and poverty. Britain was in trouble, and high among Maynard Keynes's tips to Ramsay to get the country on its feet were a reduction in wages, a reduction in unemployment benefits and, what would concern Leo more than he knew now while enjoying his long home leave, a ten per cent cut in the armed services.

All in all the Milligans would be glad to get back to Burma. The boys hated the restrictions imposed on whites in Catford and not just because:

> England didn't have any chocolate trees, candy mountains or ice-cream bushes. She had weather: lots of it, and mostly bad. Long queues of unemployed men and as many public beggars as were ever seen in the streets of Bombay. I spent twelve months longing for the clear skies of Rangoon, and the end of our vacation couldn't come quickly enough for me and Desmond. England? Oh God!

Nine England Home and Beauty

*Ill fares the land to hastening
ills a prey where wealth accumulates
and men decay.*

Goldsmith

When Spike thought about the land of his youth he didn't remember there being much green in India or Burma. They had a
garden and the gardener was called a *mali*. Milligan knew he
came from somewhere but he didn't know where:

> *He used to evaporate and then reappear every evening. On his
> shoulders he had two stoups of water which he used to empty
> over the cosmos – dahlia-like flowers of various colours. Ours
> were, if I remember rightly, pink and white.*

No, there wasn't a lot of green, now that he came to think of
it. A sort of dust-bowl agriculture. Very tough. When the monsoon came it used to go green, but then the sun would appear
and dry it out immediately. Nine months of the year, the sun;
and the monsoon was measured in weeks – that was, like, the
winter. Yet even the rain was hot. It would hit the *maidan* – the
ground – and you would see it steaming as it came up. Because
he was born in India his blood was thin and geared to it, so he
never noticed the heat:

> *I loved it. I think I must have felt my life out there.*

And yet green is very important to Milligan. When he was
very small his mother gave him a green ribbon with a little brown
badge of Ireland's patron saint, and every St Patrick's Day she
pinned this green ribbon on his shirt.

> *It often breaks my heart to think I lost it. Still, I have it in my
> head and it can hardly escape from there – can it?*

The Rangoon to which Spike Milligan returned from disap-
pointing England was paradise. He was happy to be back in

school with the de La Salles. His brother Desmond was on familiar ground, secure. Flo was her own mistress in the Brigade House once more and Leo had even more ambitious plans for more ambitious shows. Better than that, they were what few working-class folk could be in England – privileged proletarians – or are soldiers the original 'lumpen' proletariat?

Spike's Aunt Eileen became engaged to an engineer and they planned to set up home in the old Milligan house in Kirkee. It would have to be redecorated and she gently but firmly spurned Leo's offer of help with the decor. Her brother-in-law's experience with paint was less than successful. Years before, Grandfather Kettleband had recruited him to give a hand with decorating the house in Poona. Leo started while the family were attending Mass one Sunday at St Patrick's Cathedral.

Spike says it was pure slapstick. He kept putting his foot in the whitewash and, in the end, even tipped the bucket over himself from the top of the ladder. When the family were coming back from chapel in a tonga, this white spectre passed them, going in the opposite direction on a bicycle. Flo recognized this man covered in whitewash and said, 'Wait a minute, Leo!'

> He said, 'Don't stop me! Don't stop me! I must get to St Patrick's for holy water!' He brought it back and threw it round the room because he thought the devil was in the house with him. As he flung the holy water he kept blessing himself and saying devoutly, 'That'll get rid of the bastard!'

Eileen, it seems generally agreed, was one of the most beautiful women in India. It was 1933 when she fell in love with the engineer named Brian McIntyre. Until then she had never taken boyfriends very seriously at all. Spike remembered when his aunt was keeping company with a Sergeant Keith of the Royal Ulster Rifles. Milligan took a mischievous delight in playing gooseberry:

> One moonlight night, they were sitting in the garden and I was stringing my ukulele. This Sergeant Keith, being Irish, suddenly bent down in front of Eileen and started to kiss her hand and her arm right up to the elbow. Then he said to me, 'Now lad, can you play, "I'll be Loving You Always"?'

Milligan was only seven at the time:

> Off I went, and he started, like gravel on a shovel, 'I'll behee

*loving you alwahays . . .' And then, 'Can yeh give me a
different key, please?' So we spent about five minutes in the
kneeling position with him holding this embarrassed girl's hand
and me trying to work out the right key for him to sing the song
in. It was so ridiculous!*

He interrupts himself and laughs:

*Why did I make a point about the sergeant being Irish? Well,
you know how one memory prompts another? I shared an office
in Soho onetime with Mike and Bernie Winters. The floor
above was rented to a prostitute and, when we had nothing to
do – which in those days was always – we used to time the
clients. One day I asked the lady who were the worst and best
customers. 'The English,' she said, 'are the best, because they
are so ashamed of what they're doing they want to get in and
out as quickly as possible. The Irish are the worst because they
want to kiss us as well!' The poor romantic Irish, to them a
lady is a lady, whatever her rank or profession.*

Spike was thirteen when Eileen became engaged to McIntyre,
whom Milligan liked. This was important to Milligan because
Eileen, only a few years his senior, seemed more like a sister to
him than an aunt.

Leo Milligan was forty-three when he received notice of discharge from the Forces. He protested and pleaded, but the army
was adamant; he was one of the ten per cent who were to be made
redundant. Spike says his father always blamed 'the socialists',
despite the fact that Ramsay MacDonald, as Prime Minister in
the National Government, was never any more than a hostage to
the Tories.

*All Dad knew was that it was a socialist Prime Minister who
fired him and cut the army by ten per cent.*

Job or no job, Leo decided, the show must go on. He and Flo
did a last gig for the army before leaving Rangoon. They even
roped in Spike. 'Dressed up as a page in a red uniform with blue
buttons and a pill-box cap', he presented flowers to the female
artistes.

Troopers to the end, they didn't let the grease-paint run but,
remembering, no doubt, the Irish admonition in adversity that
'God is good', they held back the tears and packed for England,

63

home, and beauty. They would spend a few days with the Kettlebands of Poona before bidding goodbye to India for the last time.

On 24th April, 1933, they left Rangoon. It rained very heavily as they sailed down the Irrawaddy River; the Shwe Dagon Pagoda and the other familiar landmarks were lost in the mists of rain:

> *I cried bitterly at leaving but never let anyone see me. I was just fifteen.*

For Spike it was heart-breaking. Along the Irrawaddy, he could almost feel the landmarks that were hidden in the mists. Above all, the rain. And the whole landscape of Rangoon now a grey mist, and he cried and cried and ran down to the cabin so that nobody would see his tears. He was going to lose his friends:

> *. . . and my friendships are on a bed of love . . . Jumbo Day and his brother; Tommy Beasley . . . and all the friends of schooldays.*

He was leaving them behind, never to see them again:

> *I never went back to India because I couldn't bear the sadness of it. I had only recently seen the misery of England in 1931. I thought it was awful at the time, though since then I've changed my mind and I now think it's terrible.*

To this day he feels that somebody somewhere stole his childhood before it had run its natural course. In 1959 he wrote 'Indian Boyhood':

> *What happened to the boy I was?*
> *Why did he run away?*
> *   And leave me old and thinking, like*
> *There'd been no yesterday?*
> *   What happened then?*
> *Was I that boy*
> *   Who laughed and swam in the bund?*
> *Is there no going back?*
> *   No recompense?*
> *Is there nothing?*
> *   No refund?*[1]

Later in 1933 the British Raj in general, and theosophists in particular, mourned the temporary passing of Annie Besant. With her death, and the popular rejection of Mahatma Gandhi, they became convinced that the Nehrus, father and daughter, would murder them all in their beds. Annie Besant died for a while at Adyar, Madras, on the 20th September, 1933, confident that she would be immediately reincarnated and sent back to the life assigned to her by the occult hierarchy.

Meanwhile, during their last days in Poona, Spike and his brother, Desmond, were taken to see Boris Karloff in *The Mummy*. Spike remembers the film because it seemed so strange that there were no horses or guns, or sheriffs or posses or bankrobbers:

> We knew more about the culture of the Wild West than we did about India. We used to play Cowboys and Indians all the time – in India for God's sake! My father had me indoctrinated.
> I've shot my family so many times in every room of the house. I remember my grandmother would be telling me a tale and suddenly I'd go, 'Bang, you're dead!'

His father remained enchanted by cowboys until the day he died, and with a shake of the head Spike asks rhetorically, 'Isn't that amazing?' In the sixties he and Leo went for a walk in Australia. There was a lovely mountain behind Leo's house on which he used to gaze and, beyond the mountain, wonderful bush country. He had never walked there. So Spike took him exploring, in a Land Rover:

> We had a drink in a pretty wild pub there, and in the distance we could see smoke rising out of the hills. Immediately he cried, 'Navajo!' and he was eighty-seven then.

But, when he and Desmond came out of the Empire cinema in Poona, Spike knew that what they called the 'Golden Years' were finished – kaput. They weren't going to any land of chocolate ice cream, he knew that now. They were leaving the real Aladdin's Cave behind and going to England to see the pantomime.

The boys were deeply depressed at the prospect, but nothing could dampen Flo's excitement at the promise in store. Spike is filled with warm admiration for his parents and the way they put aside their own worries about unemployment. Just as soon as the ship, the *Rajputana*, slipped out of Bombay for London via

Aden, Suez and Marseilles, they threw themselves into organizing ship concerts for the rest of the passengers:

> My mother was truly excited. She and Father were just
> marvellous in the way they seemed to take whatever life sent
> along. They forgot about leaving the army and being so upset
> about it. They didn't worry about the future in England in the
> depression of the thirties. I don't think they even knew what
> was in store for them. They were going home to England. It
> wasn't costing them anything, and they were determined to
> enjoy it. My mother sent sheaves of post-cards to England –
> and back to India – showing pictures of the ship. She wrote on
> the cards and marked them to show their excellent cabins. She
> was in her element.

Poverty, it has been said, could be explained by the varying number of dependants a worker has to support during his lifetime taken in relation to his varying earning power from youth to old age. By all accounts Spike's father, in the England of the early and middle thirties, should have been a well-off working man. His pension was fifty shillings per week, at a time when the wage for a first-class tradesman was barely in excess of two pounds and a man on the newly cut dole could expect less than a pound per week to keep his family.

Leo felt like a pauper. He began to miss the perks of India and realize the value of the 'all found' life of the professional soldier, now gone for good. But he and Flo were tough customers and they knew that the only way to meet 'adversity' was head-on. He didn't sit and mope about his misfortune but contented himself with throwing a few well-chosen expletives in the direction of the establishment before getting down to the business of writing yet another job application.

Flo knew that she was never going to have another place like the Brigade House but she buckled down to making No 4, Riseldine Road, Catford, as like 15, Godwin Road, Rangoon, as Leo's pension would allow.

Yet, because the England of the day was a bit like the curate's egg, there was hope for even the most lowly Londoner:

> . . . It would be quite wrong to think of unemployment as being
> endemic throughout the country. It was confined to those regions
> that were heavily dependent on the old staple industries so

1a Spike Milligan's parents relax outside
their army bungalow. Kirkee, India, 1922.

b Spike Milligan is on the left,
his brother Desmond second from the right.
The little boy at the end of the line
was the son of Desmond's ayah. Rangoon, India, 1932.

2 Spike Milligan. Photograph from the BBC radio programme *The Goons* © 1958.

3a Spike Milligan, Peter Sellers and Harry Secombe in *The Goon Show*. 1954.

b Spike Milligan, Harry Secombe and Peter Sellers together after twelve years in a one-performance revival recording of *The Goon Show*. 1 May 1972.

4a Prince Charles, a great fan of the Goons,
paid a private visit to Peter Sellers' home
in Elstead, Surrey. Summer 1964.

b Spike Milligan with Eric Sykes. November 1984.

5a Spike Milligan with his art exhibition in aid of
the Family Planning Association. 10 August 1965.

b Spike Milligan takes a petition to 10, Downing Street
on behalf of Compassion in World Farming and of Animals Vigilantes
for the abolition of the battery cage. 11 December 1979.

6 Spike Milligan addresses a rally organized by Greenpeace
in protest of the Canadian seal hunt. 3 November 1978.

7 Spike Milligan as Ben Gunn in *Treasure Island*,
with J. S. Taylor playing Jim Hawkins. 12 December 1974.

8 *Aquarius:* 'Milligan 'N' Melly'. 16 September 1973.

drastically contracted in the 1930s. Thus Jarrow, a small
shipbuilding town on the River Tyne near Newcastle, relied
almost completely on a firm that was closed down in 1934; in
1935 nearly three-quarters of the insured workers in Jarrow
were out of work.[2]

Leo got a job as a reporter with Associated Press, Desmond
went to school, and Spike was sent to study metal-work at the
South-East London Polytechnic where he learned little 'except
what boys used to do to themselves and each other'. Leo was
still keeping the family happy with his apocryphal biography
even though Spike was beginning to question the veracity of all
his father recounted:

> *He was, of course, a total romantic. Growing up I'd all these*
> *terrific stories he told me about fighting tigers bare-handed and*
> *that. Riding with Quantro's Guerillas in Mexico or with Doc*
> *Holliday through Dakota were among his least fanciful*
> *experiences. Well, no good Catholic boy likes to doubt the word*
> *of his father, but I worked out eventually that he must have*
> *been all of two when he started robbing trains with the James*
> *Gang (though maybe he might have started early for you*
> *never can tell with the Irish). And I said to him, 'Dad, all*
> *these stories you've always told – they're all lies?' He said,*
> *'Yes, that's right, but what would you rather have, Terry,*
> *an exciting lie, or a boring truth?'*

For a while, Leo thought of going on the British stage but Flo
was bitterly opposed to the notion. From now on he would act
her age and that was that. Leo had to turn down many offers
because Flo threatened to leave him if he persisted in show business. They were in the real world now; it was time to put away
play-things of tinsel-town and buckle down to the seriousness of
civilian life.

Ten The Wonderful World of Want

Work hard and God will love you. The devil doesn't care.

Connolly and Stephens, *Lessons in Reality*

Leo did all the things for his kids that a father and mother should do, and Flo cuddled Spike or beat him as her mood dictated. She never realized that Spike was good at drawing and English; and only his Uncle Hughie apparently knew that Spike had a great gift for music.

Spike wanted folk to be happy and, while very young, he discovered that he could make people laugh by doing things out of the ordinary, such as when he joined the school cast of a nativity play dressed as a clown and carrying a spear.

Then, during the trip home to Tilbury, he did a magic show aboard ship assisted by young Desmond. Flo and Leo were not ignoring the progress of their eldest son. They would, as 'Gorden and Gann', have noticed – had he been famous. Leo would have noticed his talented son earlier but he had been busy noticing Flo who was preoccupied noticing herself.

England was a culture-shock which Dante must have had in mind as the prototype for some place or other. The Milligans hid themselves away from their 'common' neighbours – enclosed in an island tenement surrounded by slums. Leo and his boys lived in a world peopled from day-dreams with characters from fantasy. They spoke the same language as English boys, they dressed like them too, but they were strangers in a foreign country.

Desmond was proving himself to be a fine artist, and it was now in their attic 'hermitage' that he and Spike began to play together at the serious business of making and illustrating stories. Gently, almost imperceptibly, Leo guided and encouraged their efforts while Flo entered their room only to change the bed linen.

On returning to reality, one might think that Flo Milligan

would have had the time to stand and stare in the direction of her son's literary, musical and theatrical ambitions. But that was not to be the case. It was goodbye to all that. There would be no more soldiering, no more concert parties, no more 'Gwen Gorden and Leo Gann'. In so far as Mrs Milligan was concerned, art, like 'Gorden and Gann', was with Leo's pay-book in India:

> She knew that Dad was hankering all the time to get back in front of the footlights. But she had decided that if she was not going to cavort about the stage, neither was he. God help him: I still have his dancing mat and make-up case.

It took them time to come to terms with insecurity and indeed it took a war and a lot of living before they accepted that any change at all had taken place.

The Milligans were at more of a disadvantage because the army manual had never mentioned poverty, and since the job of the soldier is death, life got scant attention from the military men. Then, too, it had been an unwritten law that soldiers and NCOs share the same politics as the King, but the Milligans were no longer governed by rules that protected lords, monarchs and madmen. For the first time they would, whether they liked it or not, become politically aware.

To Spike, throughout his life, the solution has always been quite simple: all the world has to do is enact the teachings of Christ. In June, 1963, for example, we find him complaining, in a letter to *The Times*, that Christians were not practising Christianity:

> Christians are turned out as though from a mould, size is no substitute for quality. I myself was baptized a Catholic, and I still don't know what it's all about, nobody ever bothered to teach me. Year after year I listen for a message of enlightenment from the pulpit, but no, the Gospels, the Epistles, are repeated ad nauseam, but of contemporary guidance there is nothing. Going around saying, 'And the Lord said unto Moses' won't get us anywhere. Jesus didn't talk about throwing the money lenders out of the Temple, he did it, then talked.[1]

Catford, barely across the river from the Milligan stomping ground of Poplar, was marginally on the 'swede bashers' bank of the Thames. From Lewisham High Street to the Mile End Road, when folk wanted to see a play or look at the pictures in the Tate or the National Art Gallery, they spoke of 'going up West', and put on their Sunday clothes to visit another country, which indeed the West End of London was.

Not many ever did go up West. They had no reason to. Nor did they need sociologists to tell them about themselves. They knew what they were, who knew better? They were Irish Catholics and Scots refugees from poverty, heathen Lascars on the run from maritime slavery, *émigré* Jews escaping from the pogroms of Czarist Russia, and French Protestants. They were also disadvantaged English people with the same right to be poor as anybody else.

Their religions, occupations or places of origin were their distinguishing features – 'Irish bastard', 'Jewish bastard', 'Nigger bastard'; there were even a few 'Froggie bastards' who hadn't made it 'up West' with the rest of the Huguenots. Appellations applicably acceptable to people who knew the full extent of each other's poverty and pride.

But the working class call each other derogatory names only in anger. 'Cock' and 'Luv' are much more common. It was the folk from 'up West' who saw a profit in religious and racial discrimination. Sixth Baronet, Sir Oswald Mosley, from soap boxes all over the East End, asked the people of Stepney and Shoreditch to view each other with suspicion.

In 1932 Sir Oswald became leader of the British Union of Fascists. With the support of Lord Rothermere and his *Daily Mail* he began to pronounce on religious differences, apartheid, the 'purity' of the 'Aryan People' and the 'destiny of the British super-race'.

After going with Desmond and his parents to bathe at his Aunt Kathleen's house in Newquay Road, Catford, Spike's weekends would have been spent in streets which were the scenes of constant running battles between the British Union of Fascists, the National Socialist League (formed by the notorious Lord Haw-Haw) and Arnold Leese's Imperial Fascist League on one side, and the Anti-Fascist Alliance on the other. Spike went on the anti-fascist marches and there isn't any doubt about Leo's feelings at the time:

> *Dad was a socialist, even if he didn't subscribe to politics until after he had been flung out of the army by the very people he thought he owed allegiance to. They made this thing called the*

'ten per cent cut'. They cut everything by ten per cent – the army, the navy, they even cut ten per cent off the old man's leg, but he was a solid socialist. Of course he was working as a journalist in Fleet Street at the time. He worked seven days a week. I remember he'd leave at about six in the morning and wouldn't return home until after eleven at night. He was a working man. Of course he was a socialist.

Spike stayed at the polytechnic for about a year, but he couldn't see it enhancing his prospects greatly so he decided to look for a job. The tech would get calls for young people so Spike applied:

Having studied metal-work I got a job with Stones of Deptford as a book-keeper! I was no good at book-keeping at all! The firm must have lost thousands! I was there about a year and a half and I was so bored with it all. They just said, 'Well, you're no good at book-keeping, are you?' So they gave me a job where I tested fuse boxes. Having nearly electrocuted myself, they sacked me.

It is a popularly held belief that armies, prisons and unemployment create unemployable people. In the case of Leo Milligan, nothing could be farther from the truth. Having after much trial and tribulation got a job where he was now working, as the saying has it, 'Three nights on a Sunday', he applied to his bosses, Associated Press, for an extra job as a news photographer's agent, and got it.

Indeed, even before he had any job, before any of his prayers or applications had been answered, he rose each morning, got the workman's tram and scoured the city for work. Spike remembers in *Open Heart University*:

'Catford 1933'

The light creaks
    and escalates to rusty dawn
The iron stove ignites the freezing
    room.
Last night's dinner cast off
    popples in the embers.
My mother lives in a steaming sink.
Boiled haddock condenses on my plate
    Its body cries for the sea.

> *My father is shouldering his braces*
> *   like a rifle,*
> *And brushes the crumbling surface of*
> *   his suit.*
> *The* Daily Herald *lays jaundiced on*
> *   the table.*
> *'Jimmy Maxton speaks in Hyde Park'.*
>
> *My father places his unemployment*
> *   cards in his wallet – there's*
> *plenty of room for them.*
> *In greaseproof paper my mother wraps*
> *   my banana sandwiches.*
> *It's 5.40. Ten minutes to catch that*
> *   last workman's tram.*
> *Who's the last workman? Is it me?*
> *   I might be famous.*
> *My father and I walk out and are*
> *   eaten by yellow freezing fog.*
> *Somewhere, the Prince of Wales*
> *   and Mrs Simpson are having*
> *   morning tea in bed.*
> *God Save the King*
> *But God help the rest of us.*[2]

With Leo working as a journalist and a photographer's agent for the A.P., together with his army pension, he must have been on about eight pounds per week, and thirty pounds a month was a sizable wage before the war. And yet he never thought of himself as anything other than a member of the proletariat. Spike says he still went on buying the *Daily Herald*:

> *He'd say, ''Tis a terrible paper, this!' And he'd go on ordering it for another year! I couldn't understand his attitude. He knew he had to be working class. Wasn't there a great loyalty in that?*

1935 saw the beginning of the end of the Liberal Party and a partial resurgence in the fortunes of Labour. The November General Election returned 387 Conservatives, 154 Labour, and only 17 Liberal Members of Parliament. Ramsay MacDonald stood against Emanuel Shinwell in the Seaham Harbour constituency, and Manny told me:

I absolutely trounced him and have never enjoyed such political satisfaction before or since.[3]

In June 1936, a Popular Front Government came to power in Spain. On 17th July, a detachment of the Spanish Army, under General Francisco Franco Bahamonde, mutinied, The rebellion spread to the mainland and, within forty-eight hours, the whole country was plunged into civil war.

Scenes reminiscent of Berlin in the aftermath of the Reichstag fire were enacted in the streets of London. Mosley's British storm-troopers smashed up Jewish shops, terrorized residents, set fire to homes. In imitation of the notorious Nuremberg Nazi Rallies, Lord Rothermere pledged his newspapers to publicize and pay for similar demonstrations in London's Olympia.

When Mosley declared that his Black-shirted British Union of Fascists would march through the East End of London and drive out the Jews, the Anti-Fascist League declared, 'They shall not Pass.' Spike was there with, it seemed, 'the whole of the East End', waiting to welcome England's *Führer* apparent with 'a pile of cobble-stones':

> *I was a member of the Young Communist League of Brockley. And we went to Cable Street. I was at the back, throwing rocks over the top. It was madness. Complete madness. All the people who wanted a punch-up with the fascists at lunch-time were there when Mosley turned up. I wouldn't have been a fascist that day for anything!*

In 1937 Ramsay MacDonald died on board ship while on a health visit to South America. Spike remembers the year of MacDonald's death for different reasons:

> *I went to Woolwich Arsenal as a semi-skilled fitter and what I did there I wish to God I knew. You know when you get the end of a cable and you stick it into a plug? Well, here there were two cables – positive and negative. I had to turn them round in a circle and put them into a brass container that overlapped, which meant that there were two brass containers in each loop. I might have been auditioning for a part in Chaplin's* Modern Times.

He used to day-dream a lot because the job was so boring. A Mr Rose was in charge, and the apprentices had to take their work in to him to have it passed. Spike took 'this miserable effort of mine': 'D'ye call this a day's work?' Mr Rose asked. To which Milligan responded, 'Do you think I came in to do it at nights?'

Spike's main problem was that work was beginning to get in the way of the art. He had started making music, semi-professionally, the year before, and the Woolwich Arsenal was not first in his list of priorities:

> *Music made you think of important things like politics. As I said before, when we came home my father used to buy the* Daily Herald. *And I realized I was poor, my father was poor, and the people who seemed to be concerned with the poor read the* Daily Herald *or the* Daily Worker. *And, because the* Daily Worker *was an atheist paper, my mother wouldn't have it in the house. But father wanted it. More truth in it. And then I was a trades unionist, you see. General and Municipal Workers at the Woolwich Arsenal. In the end I joined the Young Communist League because I didn't think the Labour Party was getting anywhere.*

Spike first became a crooner with a dance-band called The New Era Rhythm Boys. He realized that he couldn't just sit in the band, so he learned to play the guitar.

His first choice of instrument was the trumpet, but he couldn't afford one. It was louder than other instruments, and he wanted to be heard. In a vain effort to purchase his first trumpet he commandeered some of the products from a tobacco firm, Speers and Ponds of Deptford, for whom he had worked as a packer.

> *I flogged a few fags every day until I had enough money to pay for the horn. But somebody reported me and I was brought up before this old bastard of a manager. I'll never forget it. Had me arrested. My poor mother. My poor mother? My poor father, for God's sake! Poor father? Poor bloody me! I'll never forget that terrible man as long as I live. Got my own back years afterwards. I wrote him into* The Goons.

When the case came to court, Spike didn't have a defending solicitor – the family couldn't afford one. But that didn't mean he was on his own. Leo made a suberb plea to the magistrate, in which he said that his son was a great worker and very good to his mother. He was really an artist, who needed a trumpet and saw no other way of obtaining one except by stealing. He would become a successful musician and, in due course, repay every penny.

It was a brilliant and incredible defence, which Spike witnessed his father rehearsing in front of a mirror at home the night before the trial. Brilliant because it persuaded the magistrate to deal leniently with his son; incredible, because he sought to achieve his son's acquittal on a charge of pilfering, by proving that Spike was really a thief:

> Dad made an impassioned plea. It went, 'Here's a talented boy whose musical talent is now enjoyed by dancers all round the South-Eastern area. But for his stealing they would not have had it. And I propose to repay every penny.' Oh, he loved it. One of the best parts he ever played. He put everything into it. He put on the good suit and dropped his voice two tones until it sounded like Donald Wolfit, and he held the court spellbound for about ten minutes. They were just happy to say, 'Not guilty', glad to get him out of the bloody way before he asked for an arts grant from the poor-box.

It could have been scripted by Molière, and indeed the first *Goon Show* that Spike wrote makes fun of the incident by having the defendant charged with being in possession of 'two thousand half-smoked cigarettes'. Exhilarated by the victory, Leo and Spike jumped on a passing tram only to be put off at the next stop because neither had the fare home. As Max Miller said, 'I only have to look at my wife's curlers to realize that every climax has its anti-climax.'

I asked Milligan how he came to be called Spike:

> In those days we used to listen to Radio Luxembourg, and they were featuring one of the zaniest, noisiest bands anybody ever heard. They were simply crazy, and they were called 'Spike Jones and his City Slickers'. You know, I'd always wanted a public name – to hide behind, I suppose. The way my mother called me 'Terence' in a bid to make me respectable, and Dad said 'Terry', like I was some sort of chocolate. Soon the other guys began to call me Spike, and I loved it.

According to Spike's pre-war jobs he was a jack-of-all-trades: book-keeping, engineering, tobacco-packaging – whatever they were doing around the South-East of London, Spike Milligan did his share. But the most educational by far must have been working as a junior assistant at Chislehurst Laundry. Working so close to a mainly female workforce has to be one of the most liberating experiences for any young man. If an adolescent is still a virgin when he leaves a laundry, he will at least have been left in no doubt about the delights the future has in store for him. But:

> *What's a junior assistant, for Christ's sake. A quid a week, and double-meaning talk from young girls that makes an old man happy but scares the pants off a frightened young boy. And you couldn't possibly know how dangerous a laundry could be – death-traps they were. I remember they had this great calender for the clothes; a bloody big drum of a thing that used to go its own way – everybody was terrified to go near it. Apart from the shit, it was positively frightening. Everything in that laundry seemed to lead a life of its own. Then there was this machine for folding cardboard into packets. Inside, a big guillotine used to fly around like a bloody dervish, slicing up the card.*

One day it stopped, and Spike looked inside. Without warning it started again and all but scalped him! When he reported the incident to the charge-hand he was sacked!

> *If we'd known we could have sued them because there was no guard on the machine. But we were so ignorant in those days – all working people were.*

And then, as if profundity might bore us all, he turns to his favourite fall guy, Spike Milligan, and tells you how he donned this stupid-looking cap for which he had to get a special dispensation from the priest so as to wear it at Mass. He insists that his ears weren't big enough to hold his cap up – the trouble being that since the working class, he said, couldn't afford to buy caps by the size, they bought them by weight, depending on how many kids they had. And this one used to come down over Spike's eyebrows:

> *So I used to go round with this ridiculous cap on. I'd sit in the back of the chapel so that people wouldn't see me and I'd run out before the Mass would be over. It was in that laundry my first girl-friend worked, Nina Hall. I was in love with her, but then I've loved all the women I've ever liked. Romantic? She*

didn't want to be seen out with me in this crazy head-gear.
Love me love my cap! I lost my hair, my job, and my
girl-friend.

He couldn't be happy in dead-end jobs. And although his
father tried to grin and bear it, England was proving poor com-
pensation for the loss of India where the most lowly member of
the rank and file had servants to come and shave him, clean his
shoes, wash his clothes! Everything had been done for him.

What had they got in Catford?

The 'workman's' tram! The 'workman's' tram was like . . . let
me see. You know the ship that takes you across the River
Styx to the Underworld? This was the duplicate! Six o'clock
in the morning in seering yellow fog he had to be up to catch the
first 'workman's'. He got a penny off the return fare. It was a
cruel thing to do. Imagine. To force the poor to get up at that
time in the morning to save a halfpenny each way. Outrageous!

Eleven Love's Young Dream

When all the world is young, lad,
And all the trees are green,
When every goose is a swan, my lad,
And every lass a queen.

A. E. Housman

His mother worked so hard, and his father so seldom complained, that Spike shoved India to the back of his mind and got on with the job of living.

He felt that the guitar wasn't big enough, so 'when this guy in the band got fed up playing the double-bass, I bought it'. Having taught himself how to play it he decided, 'Milligan, this is too big, you know.'

Getting it on and off public transport was not so much a problem as a pantomime. He had to get it to the front of the tram, where luggage was normally placed, and then run like the wind to get back on the car himself in case the vehicle moved off, or he was killed by another tram coming from the opposite direction.

The dance-hall where he played was opposite the gates of Brockley cemetery and, as he alighted, every tram-driver would say the same thing: 'Wot yeh goin' ter do wiv that then – bury it?' In the end it got so that Spike couldn't stand it any more, so he used to rush up to the front of the tram, grab his double-bass and shout at the tram-driver, before he had a chance to say a word: 'No, mate, I'm not going to bleeding bury it!'

Although Milligan didn't know it then, he was really serving his apprenticeship to literature more than music. But it's a great way to learn how to write. Use everything. Use every experience. Let form take shape and shape make form. Milligan did and saw Jesus through the double-bass:

> *I thought I saw Jesus on a tram.*
> *I said, 'Are you Jesus?'*
> *He said, 'Yes I am.'* [1]

James Thurber said that his cousin learned by literary correspondence that he would never be a writer. Thurber could never make up his mind if that was a good or a bad thing – on the one hand he approved of education, on the other he firmly believed that nothing should interfere with natural stupidity. Spike Milligan was never even aware that people needed teaching in the putting together of words. He is derived from the old school that predated Dr Johnson, unafraid to end a sentence with a preposition, doubling his negatives with the best, or splitting an infinitive with all the expertise of an Einstein declaring war on an atom.

Milligan did, however, attend Goldsmith's College of Music in Lewisham Way, and said it was the nearest thing he ever had to a musical education. He went to 'get the dots', more or less, and claims to have learned about the double-bass at evening classes. He didn't like Goldsmith's because, it was 'all classical music' and, at the time, he only wanted to play jazz. So it was that he remembered only what he thought might be useful to him – notation and fingering.

He also learned how to bow a little. And that was something he hadn't known about at all, since most of the 'anti-musical' double-bass players just strum and play pizzicato:

> I used to imagine the bloke who sold it to me trying to get it
> under his chin like a violin, before deciding that the bow must
> have been left in the case by mistake.

Because Milligan is constantly thinking through his eyes, speech is not always able to keep up with his thoughts. When he does speak you gradually become aware of the organized chaos of the mind that is capable of creating *The Goon Show* and *Puckoon*, or writing the most delicate verse.

The harnessing of the manic state Milligan sees as 'mastering the mania'. Nowadays we are told that most creative people must suffer from some self-destructive urge that connotes intellect with genius: Jeffrey Meyers calls it paradoxically 'The Dynamics of Destruction' and in his work, *Manic Power*, quotes Byron:

> There is something I am convinced in the poetical temperament
> that precludes happiness, not only to the person who has it, but
> to those connected with him.[2]

Milligan saw it like that too. In his poem 'Manic Depression', he writes:

The pain is too much
A thousand grim winters grow in my head
In my ears
> *the sound of the*
>> *coming dead.*

All seasons, all same
> *All living*
> *All pain*
No opiate to lock still
> *my senses.*
Only left the body locked tenser.[3]

With Spike the manic state takes many forms, mainly obsessional. He expects folk to do as he would: always on time, he abhors unpunctuality, and yet time or history is only relevant to the theme of his conversation:

> *I was with Jack Fallon, the bass player, a few days ago when*
> *he was doing a gig at Eastbourne. Irish-Canadian. He was*
> *born in a log cabin, would you believe – like Lincoln. I'd never*
> *met anyone who was born in a log cabin.*

Fallon is from his past. He first met him when he was playing with the 'Bill Hall Trio' at Churchill's night-club in Bond Street. In those days, Fallon was with the Jack Jackson band.

He liked the big Irish-Canadian musician from the first time they met:

> *Apart from being a great bass player, he's a superb*
> *conversationalist. He's such an intelligent man – which is not,*
> *as you know, the case with all musicians; brains are not*
> *compulsory. I call that condition 'the duo personality'; a chap*
> *will play a divine instrument and, when he stops, he will*
> *talk like an idiot. Even praising some of them can be like a*
> *panegyric – talking over a dead body.*

Yet, sometimes, it's as if words, too, get in the way of this speech:

> *Anyway, Jack Fallon was the other night bowing like a man*
> *possessed – col arco it's called, we call it arco, with the bow.*
> *Col legno means 'on the wood'. Fallon did a whole chorus with*
> *the bow and singing in unison with what he was playing – like*

*'Slim and Slam', the American couple who used to play the
double-bass and, as they played, they sang along. Jack was
inspired and knew exactly what note he was going to hit.
Almost spiritual – no words to describe the feeling. . . .*

On 3rd June, 1937, American divorcee Wallis Simpson wed
the newly created Duke of Windsor in France and, while on
their honeymoon, the former King was informed that his wife
was to be excluded from enjoying her husband's rank. The title
of royal highness was for himself alone. Spike, too, decided to
abdicate his responsibility for fitting battery leads to somebody
else. Although now earning as much at the Woolwich Arsenal as
his father was getting as a journalist, Spike still thought of
manual work as the curse of the artist.

His mother hated what he did with the band and he hated
what she wanted him to do. He agrees that he and his friends,
with their Brylcreemed hair and Roaring Twenties attitudes,
must have looked a sight whenever Flo saw them together, but
'when', Spike argues, 'did kids ever look right to their parents?'

*Didn't somebody say that we are all of us the children our
mothers wouldn't let us play with?*

Desmond and Spike had never been able to invite friends into
the house. Spike wasn't even encouraged to bring his girl-friends
home. 'Though when making music took most of my time, Dad
was good about me staying out all night on gigs and so on. He
just told Mother that I always saw to her money first, whether I
was working at a 'real' job or not: 'He's bringing home the dibs,
my dear. He's bringing home the dibs.'

*Successful? Yes, I guess we were successful. Were we any good?
We were serving our time, so I suppose we were as good as any
other apprentices. What we lacked in technique we made up for
in enthusiasm. We were the Harlem Club Band, we were able
to keep time, and dancers didn't ask for a great deal more. We
drew the crowds and they thought we were fine.*

They pulled the birds, too. Never in history has there been a
guy in the public eye who didn't get more than his fair share of
attention from the young kids who followed the band, and a
good-looking bass player like Milligan was not going to be the
first exception.

Milligan's 'special' girl he refers to as Lily Gibbs and, as they say in Ireland, she set her cap at Spike. But Flo's proud aloofness set problems for her son's romance. Poverty generates so much pride that it is hard to see how working-class children ever meet up with anybody even as poor as themselves. Visiting is not encouraged, since even the most frugal unbudgeted meal at night may well be tomorrow morning's breakfast. Besides which, most working-class mothers worry that losing a son might mean gaining another mouth to feed.

Spike has wondered all his life why, when Flo knew that Lily was his girl-friend, she only reluctantly and very belatedly invited her to tea at Riseldine Road. He never realized that in India Flo had been one of the privileged ex-pats and, strong and proud as she was in putting the sub-continent and all the perks behind her, there was no way that she was going to encourage 'folk' to see the Milligans in the 'reduced' circumstances they endured at Catford. Being thought of as penniless doesn't worry the rich, they don't know about poverty – being reared in the belief that God made the poor and it is blasphemous to interfere with Heaven's handiwork. To be poor, however, destroys the illusion of life and makes living precarious.

Spike recalls that time with a tinge of bitterness. He remembers that his mother did plenty of entertaining in India. He believes that should have made her much more amenable to the idea of having 'folk' in now.

But Spike's memories of boyhood as a young gentleman probably encouraged him to ignore his poverty while Flo's recollections of an impoverished childhood could never allow her to forget that she was once better off. Then, too, during the eighteen months or so that he kept company with Lily Gibbs, he didn't do any regular work. He was learning the first prerequisite of the creative artist, to eschew servitude with all the disdain that your intellect can generate.

Flo would never have understood that; she had been conditioned to accept a society in which most people worked and a few didn't. Not only was her eldest son not going to work: he was now making a stand against going to Mass! Flo was increasingly worried that he was becoming careless about the sacraments. Spike told me one time that only practising Catholics needed to be so particular. He was a time-served RC, he knew it all. One thing to worry about may be somebody like his uncle

Alf Thurgar – a convert who jumped the dyke: 'But surely,' Spike demanded, 'the one true church could show a bit of faith in one of their own?'

Alf was married to Leo's sister Kathleen, and although the Thurgars weren't rich they were comfortably off; which has less to do with wealth than relative poverty: to the poor, they appeared to be rich. Spike describes the condition as:

> *Living with the arse out of 'somebody else's trousers'. They had*
> *a bath indoors while we at Riseldine Road only had a zinc tub.*
> *Every Friday night we used to catch the 74 tram from Honor*
> *Oak Park to Catford where we changed to a 35 tram and*
> *drove all the way to 15, Bargery Road – which we thought was*
> *the other side of the world, but really it was only the other side*
> *of Catford. Then we'd each take it in turn to have a bath. It*
> *was bloody marvellous.*

And then having tea with Auntie Kathleen afterwards. It was brought in on a beautiful small oak tea-trolley 'which I have now because my cousin brought it to me when they were clearing out Aunt Kathleen's house a few years ago'. A stickler for tradition, Spike got his cousin Terry to give him a lamp that used to stand in the hall at Bargery Road and he carried it himself to his brother Desmond in Australia.

Alf Thurgar was a nice, quiet man. He was an insurance broker and he had a car that was a sign of his esteem. In the war he was an ack-ack gunner and Spike says he had a fine sense of humour for an Englishman. He was a Protestant who became a Catholic because that was the only way to get into the Milligans:

> *And, oh God, but good and all as he was converts are the worst*
> *of the lot. He became very devout and you couldn't move in*
> *his room for statues and holy pictures. Mother used to look at*
> *him and then at me without saying a word, but she didn't*
> *need to. You knew that she was thinking: If a Protestant can*
> *make such a good Catholic, where the hell did I go wrong*
> *with you?*

The act of 'jumping the dyke' fascinates Milligan, maybe because his mother's paternal side were also converts to Catholicism. He cites Graham Greene and Evelyn Waugh as examples of possessed obsessiveness. And he wonders why there:

always seems to be a literati ready to convert to Catholicism?
Sometimes, like Wilde, even on their death-beds. Oh yes,
Protestants are apt to make very serious Catholics and not at
all as funny as Oscar Wilde who, when he died in the arms of
Mother Church while drinking a bottle of champagne, told
young Queensberry, 'Bosie, I'm dying beyond my means.' Why
doesn't somebody become Jewish? Most Christians were, once.

But the world had more to worry it than bourbons, bathrooms
and bass-fiddles. Democracy was on the run. Overturned in Spain.
Ignored in Portugal. Abyssinia had been bullied into making her
trains run on time; while, in the Far East, Japan brought civilization to the Chinese and refused to take no for an answer.

Chamberlain, horrified that Germany should really want to go
to war over Czechoslovakia, wondered if he and the *Führer*
couldn't talk about this, as Adolf and the Duke of Windsor
did, like gentlemen. But the time for appeasement was over:
Hitler, convinced that he could do what he liked without fear of
British or French interference, marched into Poland on 1st September, 1939. Britain and France declared war on Germany two
days later, and Spike made love to Lily.

For seven months Chamberlain's Cabinet waged a 'phony
war' – Poland was conquered by the Germans in the first three
weeks of September. Lily Gibbs bought Spike his first trumpet
for four pounds and Leo successfully applied for a commission
in the army.

Convinced that the Second World War would be fought somewhere foreign, the British people, after the early panic over
Poland, returned to temporary normality. For a few weeks everybody had been caught up in the rush to leave Britain's cities.
But, although they sent their children to safety, the working class
stayed where they were, simply because they couldn't afford to
go. Lily Gibbs's mother was now more convinced than ever that
her daughter's boy-friend was a waster and would never be up to
a permanent and pensionable post.

Leo was becoming concerned that the *Daily Herald* was not
responding totally to the call to 'defend' poor little Poland. But
Spike knew that there were two sides to his father:

I could never get the Daily Herald *away from him because he*
was so socialist-orientated. Even when I was working, the

only way that I used to have the paper was to wrap up my sandwiches. Dad was really a bit of an Alf Garnett, you know. We'd go to a cinema and he'd say, 'Stand up for the Queen.' Then at home when mother would be going on about the 'good old days when royalty was respected,' he'd ask, 'And what did the royal family ever do for us?' Stand up for the Queen, sit down for the Queen. For Christ's sake.

Chamberlain brought Eden back into his Cabinet and gave Churchill back his old post as First Lord of the Admiralty. Very quickly the British defence forces were re-armed, and this put paid to Germany's first plans to invade the United Kingdom. Much to the annoyance of Flo Milligan, who had come to approve of Miss Gibbs's association with her son, Lily broke off her relationship with Spike on 9th April, 1940, as Germany invaded Denmark and Norway.

On 10th May, 1940 the Germans invaded Holland and Belgium and Arthur Neville Chamberlain resigned. The King commissioned Churchill to form a government and on 13th May the Labour Party ratified Attlee's decision to accept office in the new Cabinet. Churchill, as the German war machine was sweeping through Europe, told the House of Commons that he could offer the country nothing but 'blood, toil, tears and sweat'. The 'phony war' was over and the real fighting was about to begin.

Flo Milligan dominated her family with a rod of iron. If either Leo or the children didn't want to live the way she saw fit Flo could make life positively unbearable. It would have been tough on a less easy-going person than Leo, who owed far more to the optimism of Micawber than he ever did to the wrath of God. Flo stomped firmly on any show business ambitions her husband might still nurse, and she never tried to hide her dislike of her eldest son's 'rakish' progress in that field.

Milligan has never forgotten their weekly arguments. Saturday night was an especially sore point. Dance-band musicians never got home before one or two o'clock Sunday morning, and Spike was no exception. Flo would be waiting up on the landing, clock in hand, and she'd demand:

Terence! What time do you call this?

Pouring oil on troubled waters, Milligan would respond:

> *I don't call it this time, the world does! Greenwich mean time!
> One o'clock in the morning is not just my time!*

Every Saturday, according to Spike, was the same:

> *Me trying to get to bed and her trying to keep me up. 'Terence,
> you're ruining your health! It's no joke! You're ruining your
> health doing these band jobs!' I never thought of it as being
> funny. Talk about me ruining my health! Within hours she'd
> be dragging me up to catch first Mass at St Saviour's church,
> and that sort of thing didn't improve my well-being. I'd fall
> asleep in the chapel and remind her that the Sabbath was a
> day of rest. She didn't agree with that at all; real Sundays
> were for kneeling and agony, and real Catholics could make the
> day very unpleasant indeed.*

Spike couldn't stand the system and declared war on his
mother. She said he couldn't stay at home unless he attended to
his religious duties and Spike said he would practise his religion
as it suited him. Leo, caught between the black devil and the
great white God, just shook his head sadly as his son, unable to
stand any more, went to stay with friends for a while:

> *When I think of how I actually left home to escape my mother's
> vengeful Catholicism! Anyway, I didn't think God all that
> important. He never turned up when we needed Him, when we
> went around with the arses out of our trousers. I mean to say, I
> thought: What's all this praying? If it was doing us any good
> I'd understand, but nothing happened. We'd give to the church,
> and get fuckall back!*

Spike only came back to his mother's house some months later
– on his own terms. He was quite happy when he was called up in
the spring of 1940. His days in the army would be the most
enjoyable of his young life.

Twelve The Good Soldier Spike

Brothers we find our fellow men.

Friedrich Von Schiller

Spike Milligan embraced the war. His call-up papers he treated as letters of freedom. Square-bashing and weapons-training apart, he was at last free to do what all artists' devils must have time to do: nothing.

All his life he had been a keep-fit fanatic, so the army regimen wouldn't worry him. He knew all about soldiering – it had been bred in the bone: recruits carry bullets; old soldiers, grub.

Above all, he and his mother would escape from each other: for a while they could practise their own beliefs – Flo her unrelenting dogma, and Spike this new-found religion called art. Sundays had been simply horrendous.

> *In the forces the Sabbath for me was a thing of the past . . .*
> *only Protestants have souls in the British Army.*

He had always been more peasant than proletarian: India saw to that. Though he came straight from London to the Sussex countryside, he was no urban space-kid. The cantonments at Poona and Kirkee and the Brigade House in Rangoon may not have boasted green fields and rolling meadows, but even the arid *maidan* is country enough to breed a peasantry.

What he saw at Bexhill-on-Sea Milligan loved. For the first time since leaving India, he was back home. Better still, it was green. Miles and miles of grass for the walking of. Surrounded by flowers and not one of them in a window-box on a working-class sill. Spike describes the moment in *Adolf Hitler: My Part in His Downfall*:

> *At 4.30, June 2nd, 1940, on a summer's day all mare's tails and blue sky, we arrived at Bexhill-on-Sea, where I got off.*[1]

It had been a cruel thing to send a shy, sensitive boy like Milligan into the slums of Catford. Certainly millions of working-class kids all over the world wake up in thousands of Catfords all over the world and just have to grin and bear it, but they didn't get there via India. As Bill Naughton has suggested about the children of Manchester in *The Long Haul*, they were born there and never knew anywhere else. On the other hand, things rural can send Milligan into raptures:

> This was the English countryside – it sang at you – this was the reason Constable never wanted to paint anything else. The pleasures of those years were endless – from seeing a rare medlar tree, a Saxon dew-pond, an unspoilt bluebell wood, a working windmill, to watching Fred Vahey, a Sussex thatcher living in a gypsy caravan, make nettle soup from a Romany recipe.[2]

For a while he could be as rustic as he liked since it was more war-games than war the army was playing at when Spike met up with them in Bexhill-on-Sea. It seemed like a heaven-sent vacation. Absolute freedom. He remembers that he didn't have the same feeling that he used to have when he was going for a new job: then he used to feel sick in the stomach. Going into the army, he felt, was neutral. His only thought was: 'What's it going to be like?'

When his call-up papers arrived at Riseldine Road, Spike was in hospital suffering from a slipped disc so, when he arrived at the barracks in June 1940, he was three months late and wearing a suit:

> I was marched into the office in front of this Major Stokes who didn't know who I was, or why I was late, and he said, 'Why is this man in mufti?' I thought: Mufti! Does he mean I am dressed like a bloody Egyptian? The sergeant answered, 'He's been in hospital, sir.' But Major Stokes wanted to know why this recruit was wearing civilian clothes. I couldn't resist telling him, 'They won't let you in naked!'

When he heard his mouth speak, Spike asked himself, 'Why the hell did you say that?' He feels that the Irish have a sort of a death wish to be funny:

> Happily this prick of a major didn't hear anyone less important than himself. I'll never forget that meeting with Major Stokes. It was such a change coming in from the bright day outside.

He remembers it was a battery office and very stark: it had a blanket over a table, and:

> *as I described in my war book, it had a forty-watt bulb hanging from the ceiling and when you lit it, it made the room darker. They had a cut-out of Chamberlain stuck on the wall; he was holding up that sheet of Munich paper saying, 'Peace in our time.' Boy, was he wrong! How wrong can a Prime Minister get?*

In June 1940, unless they had the price of a pint and a packet of fags, the soldiers in Sussex would not have had a great deal to do but stand outside their huts, expand their chests and breathe in the countryside. They had been issued with a rifle and five rounds of ammunition apiece to hold back the Germans who might come storming up the beach at any moment, now that the army at Dunkirk was in triumphant retreat.

Since 15th May, when Holland surrendered, the news was doom-laden. Belgium threw in the towel on 28th May. And only the very day after Milligan's arrival in camp on 3rd June was the evacuation of Dunkirk completed. It had taken exactly seven days and Spike, with a comrade, actually swam in a sea of 'polished steel' at Bexhill while over on the French side the British Expeditionary Force was trying to make its way out of disaster. They swam in anxious silence and listened to the fall of France. The still summer was hardly broken by the mutter of guns firing randomly in the direction of the brave fishers of men, who had brought their little boats to the very war itself, seeking the most valuable catch they would ever net. Occasionally a squadron of Spitfires or Hurricanes headed out from England:

> *I remember so clearly, Bombardier Andrews standing up in the water, putting his hands on his hips and gazing towards where the BEF was fighting for its life. It was the first time I'd seen genuine concern on a British soldier's face. 'I can't see how they're going to get 'em out,' he said.*

Twenty-four hours later, the disaster of the previous day had become a triumph:

> *As the immensity of the defeat became apparent, somehow the evacuation turned it into a strange victory.*

The Luftwaffe had been assigned the task of 'softening up'

the United Kingdom for the invasion, and as the Battle of Britain began in July, Spike saw the planes coming in:

> *The window near my bed faced north. As I lay there, I could see the glow of the fires. The bombers were still going. Some must have been on their way back, as we heard cannon fire as night-fighters got onto them. What a bloody mess. Men in bombers raining death on defenceless civilians. . . .*

And, for a moment, Spike allowed feelings of vengeful satisfaction to intimidate his emotions as he assured himself that soon the British would be doing the same to the Germans. Getting their own back, only more so. But Milligan has never been able to stay angry with the human race for long:

> *For the love of me I couldn't get the feeling that I was part of this. Killing of civilians was an outrage I couldn't swallow on any basis, on any side. In the end there were no sides. Just living and dead.*

Because he knew that the bombers were operating in the general area of the East End Spike spent a worried night until he was able to telephone his father at his office in Fleet Street the following morning. Leo assured him that 'all was well with the family'. Indeed his father, from his vantage point, knew more about what the raid had been like than most. As a fire warden he could watch the whole of London from the top of the Associated Press building, now lit by the flames of St Paul's. Spike found it hard to understand that this was a war of words as much as bombs and bullets:

> *The papers carried stories of how many German planes were shot down, heroism of the fire brigades, wardens, Red Cross and night-fighters, etc etc. But they didn't mention the casualties. . . .*

That night Spike again wrote to Lily Gibbs as he had done assiduously since joining the army. She had broken with him but that was something Spike chose to disregard, just as he had decided to ignore the fact of Lily's new boy-friend. Milligan is, to say the least, self-willed:

> *She was the first real girl-friend I'd ever had. She was marvellous. But she got fed up waiting for me to marry her. I didn't know this at the time: anyway I didn't have any money, so marriage would*

have been out of the question. That's why she went off with
another bloke. But I carried a torch for her right through the war.

They wrote fondly to each other, and Milligan remembers that he thought it strange that she was such a 'decent straight girl because her father was a thief and her mother a drunk'.

Before the war they used to meet at London Bridge station – young people finishing work for the day:

> *And, believe it or not, it was romantic. Romantic! Meeting in*
> *that grey city by that shit-stained river that they call the*
> *Thames. 'Old Father Thames' kept rolling along poisoning*
> *the lot of us. 'Sweet Thames' Spenser called it. What's sweet*
> *about it I've got no idea; one glassful and you'd die of bleeding*
> *typhoid. They don't ever drown in the Thames – they don't ever*
> *get the chance: they just fall through and die in it. However,*
> *we used to meet there and she took a liking to me. Made a play*
> *for me, I think. Young love.*

And so it came to pass that Spike Milligan arrived in the army dressed in civilian clothes and carrying his writing materials and the trumpet bought for him by Lily Gibbs. Lily is dead now but she saved up for that instrument and that's why Milligan still has it hanging in his office.

> *War or no war, I was determined to play. She bought it, I*
> *suppose because I couldn't afford to. I gave everything to my*
> *mother. The money was all right for those days – we got ten*
> *shillings a gig . . . that wasn't a bad wage when you consider I*
> *used to do maybe three gigs a week. I used to give the lot to my*
> *mother and she'd let me have half a crown back. Lily and I*
> *would go to the pictures – a shilling each to go in and there*
> *wasn't much left of the half-crown. That was why Lily had to*
> *pay for the trumpet.*

They say that the army was unprepared for two eventualities – war and Spike Milligan. And yet, maybe his being is at total odds with his attitude. While he looks the most phlegmatic man in the world, Milligan is a go-getter, a do-er. He is a hive of innovation. Having started a proper library in the camp he decided that they should do something about music, and when the army showed reluctance Spike didn't forget about it, he just put it to one side in his mind and became the bugler's stand-in. Anything to keep his musical hand in.

And he made it his business to get to know the people in charge, for he was going to need them to make his way in the world of art and entertainment, and I choose the words carefully for, had art failed to entertain him, Milligan would be something other than an artist:

> It's very strange . . . it came in bits and pieces, like the beginning of dysentery. The first complete thing that I ever wrote was a poem in the form of a limerick about a soldier in my regiment at Bexhill-on-Sea:
>
> > There was a young bombardier called Eddser,
> > Who, when wanted, was always in bed, sir
> >
> > One morning at one they fired the gun
> > And Eddser in bed, sir, was dead, sir.

That, he says, was his first writing. He thinks he felt nothing at all. He had no idea. He hadn't been told that there was a literary world, somewhere out there. His parents didn't have a broad horizon. All they wanted was that three pounds ten a week for food, and enough to pay the rent, and that was it. Oh, and for him to come in before eleven at night.

> That was all that their world consisted of. Of course I wrote lots of letters to lots of girls and all the girls I wrote to kept my letters, believe it or not.

But, apart from blowing reveille each day, he didn't have a great deal to do until lights out but keep the Germans at bay from one of the seventy-four Martello Towers, built on the recommendation of the Duke of York to protect the most vulnerable parts of the British coastline from the threat of an invasion by Napoleon. This duke might as well have emulated his grand old ancestor and marched his men up and down the Sussex hills:

> Like Joyce and Gogarty or Abbot and Costello, here was me and Harry Edgington stationed in one to stop the entire Panzer divisions of Germany coming into England – just me and Harry Edgington and one rusty gun! I just love the thought of it: the Germans were only going to land forty thousand men; all they needed to do was aim at us to blow us out of our Martello Tower. And there we were so full of confidence, me and Harry Edgington and our machine-gun.

With few of the enemy in sight, he and the pianist soldier,

Harry Edgington, used to dabble in the written word. They both, according to Milligan, shared the same sense of humour. They started to write 'very much in the vein of *Beachcomber*. It was pretty insane, but it was a start.' The nearest Spike got to showing it to anyone of literary merit was a Lieutenant Anthony Goldsmith who had written a play with Terence Rattigan and translated a work by Flaubert. Goldsmith looked at the offering and said, 'This is mad. It's very like the Marx Brothers but it's very funny.'

> *Tony said that to me one distant day in 1942 at Robbins Post, a little concrete bunker on the Eastbourne Road. He was uselessly killed in the war, this man of great promise.*

Apart from Major Stokes who, according to Spike, was a 'fifty-six-year-old body with an eighty-nine-year-old uniform on it', the Colonel Blimps made little impression after the beginning of the war. Occasionally 'some Sandhurst shit' would turn up on parade wearing leggings and spurs, 'and the nearest horse a hundred bloody miles away!'

However, even dinosaurs like Major Stokes still had the rank to make life unpleasant for the ordinary reluctant. Spike describes Stokes's uniform as being 'all patched up with bits and pieces of leather' – that was why he got the nickname 'Major Leather Suitcase'. He used to wear riding breeches on parade, and switched a riding stock which he would whack against the side of his leg and occasionally he'd strike himself too hard and he'd go 'Oh, that smarts!'

But for the fact that Spike as a musician was one of those needed to keep morale up, he might well have become a 'Good Soldier Schweick' at the hands of Major 'Leather Suitcase':

> *The one crowd he couldn't order about was us in the dance-band, you see. Didn't know what to do about us. We'd say that if they wanted us to play at dances then they'd have to give us the mornings off to rehearse. 'Leather Suitcase' knew how we were practising but there wasn't a bloody thing he could do about it. We used to lay in bed, get our breakfast late – everything. We avoided guards because we were working at night – it was wonderful.*

Thirteen A Land Fit for Heroes

*Nothing could overcome the
Russians, fighting with passionate
devotion amid the ruins of their city.*

Winston Churchill on the Battle of Stalingrad

Spike's happiness at finding true comradeship in the army was boundless, and apart from a holy medal or a prayer-book in each letter from home, his mother couldn't get at him:

> *The sergeant-major didn't stand at the top of the stairs and say, 'Terence, where have you been, you naughty gunner?' As long as I was in, that was that. And there was nobody forcing me to go to chapel – if you didn't go to church you peeled potatoes. That was the order of he day. The NCO would scream, 'C. of E. to the church; dismiss! Roman Cat'licks, Jews and Methylated Spirits, spud peeling!' I began to think that Christ was a potato. But, the sense of emancipation! The feeling of freedom!*

Because Flo had never been able to get at Leo she had set Jesus on Spike.

For at least five of the years he had lived in Catford, Milligan's natural gregariousness was curbed to such an extent that he and Desmond had lived on the edge of his mother's moods. For him the army changed all that. Suddenly he was mixing with lots and lots of chaps who weren't jazz musicians at all.

> *Colossal spectrum of life – different accents and languages and all that. War is a lunatic situation, you know: but I thought: There's an organized sense of lunacy here, so, if we're taking part in it, we must be at least half daft. The ones who were not lunatics were called conscientious objectors. They were not lunatics because they said, 'No, we're not going to take part in it.'*

And so, he says, this lunacy started to grow on him.

> *Not that we weren't a bit crazy to begin with; after all, that*

had been implanted in me through my father's strange demeanour and manner in being a clown all the time to keep his family happy.

But there in Bexhill were all the characters Spike could ever have wanted in his life, and they were all around him.

The working-class soldier was having a better war these days. It is inconceivable that a private in Haig's army could have spoken with his 'betters' as Spike Milligan did with Anthony Goldsmith. But the scholar from Harrow and Oxford was that new breed of officer so despised by Colonel Blimp – the man with the wartime commission. The Goldsmiths of this war would get this unpleasantness over with as quickly as was humanly possible and then back to cloisters.

In the meantime, the two men were fortunate to have met. Spike introduced the literary lieutenant to a new way of looking at life and Goldsmith showed the magpie Milligan that there was another music besides jazz, and other books besides *Robinson Crusoe* and *The Swiss Family Robinson*. He taught Milligan that literature was a discipline the same as any other art form. In time, Spike even learned that wit is not the exclusive property of the working class. When the ship taking them all to the front was being strafed by Caproni bombers, Goldsmith's batman woke his sleeping superior with the information:

Sir, we are being attacked by the enemy!

Without turning, the laconic lieutenant assured his servant:

Don't worry, he's allowed to. Just make sure you get his number.

The scholar and the jack-of-all-trades were misfits among the military. Goldsmith's superiors at the beginning of the war were mainly career officers who would have had little time for a temporary subaltern who was also a Jew. By the same token, Milligan had little in common with his mates, most of whom were interested only in boozing, bawdy jokes and surrogate sex:

I loved the lads, I really loved them but I knew there was no mental food for me there.

Milligan wanted his brave new world earlier than most: to him, the army was going to become his oyster, his university.

His extra-mural studies of English and the arts would begin now, here, at Bexhill.

Besides Goldsmith, there was Lieutenant Cecil Budden, a classical pianist whose great love was Beethoven. When Milligan came in from playing jazz he would hear 'this wonderfully ranging piano coming from the big hall' of the girls' school in which they were billeted. Milligan would postpone sleep and listen to 'this officer seated at this piano in his shirt and trousers, playing Beethoven.' Spike would sit for hours, entranced:

> There I was getting a free concert at midnight when most of the others had pissed off to bed. And I learned so much from him – he was so approachable. I was able to talk to him about all aspects of music. I still do in fact: he's still a great Beethoven fiend – mad about the man.

Spike wasn't far out in his assessment of the mental capabilities of the private soldier. Between the wars little had been done for the working class of Britain. They had been left on the dole to rot, and it would be more than praiseworthy of the system to say that their education had been neglected:

> The Carnegie Trust Enquiry of 1937–9 found that of its sample of 1,800 young people aged between eighteen and twenty-five in three cities, more than a third in Glasgow were 'so deficient in physical and mental qualities' as to be totally unfit for training in a government training centre, and nearly a third in Liverpool.[1]

Cardiff was even worse. The Carnegie Trust report saw '... the operation of a vicious circle of social and economic determinism, the boy being father of the man. All things work together – education, occupational skill, home circumstance – in a conspiracy for good or evil, in terms of less or more employment, according to the status of the father.'

Times of slump had always been times of dead-end jobs and pointless 'relief employment schemes' thought up to discourage dole-taking. In the long run it was to be hoped that workers would be conditioned to accept, without protest, an even worse way of life than that which they had already endured. Nor was this condition something new; in fact Richard Hoggart in *Uses of Literacy* believed that little had changed since William Morris's day. In 1879 Morris had written:

> *I doubt if it be possible for the whole mass of men to do work in which they are driven and in which there is no hope, and no pleasure, without trying to shirk it. . . .*[2]

Mr Churchill had promised a new post-war Britain, a land really fit for heroes. But Milligan didn't want any land fit for heroes if it took desolation to create it. He never did: and he never changed his views. Years later he wrote:

> *If I die in War*
> *You remember me*
> *If I live in Peace*
> *You don't.*[3]

It was hard for an intelligent man to ignore the real state of relations between so-called friends. One had to view the friendship professed for each other by Britain and the USA with at least the slightest touch of cynicism. Everything had a price and everybody wanted value for their investment.

In the summer of 1941, after Churchill had agreed to the American occupation of Iceland, the US Navy began to patrol more widely in the Atlantic. The Lend-Lease Act, agreed to in March, was now providing more money for Britain to buy more arms to prosecute the war. True, the actual hand-over of monies and military assistance was a bit slow, but at least it seemed to show that America was going to come down eventually on the side of the good guys.

When, in the autumn of 1941, Hitler decided to defer the invasion of Britain, Churchill was in no doubt as to what had caused this change of mind. He said of the RAF: 'Never in the field of human conflict was so much owed by so many to so few.' This was no empty rhetoric: thanks to the determination and skill of the air force and the invention of radar for advance detection, Britain was not to be the 'chicken's neck' that the *Führer* boasted he would wring.

Milligan says, sarcastically, that there was a special class at Sandhurst to coach officers in the etiquette of surrender, and indeed, where the British Army itself had engaged the enemy in combat, victory was not a frequent topic for conversation until the North African campaign started. Why the government chose to do battle in that particular area was a mystery to most military minds.

Everybody knew why Italy had entered the war: it was because Mussolini at last believed that there was a chance of an Axis victory and, despite his army's reluctance and ill-preparedness, if the founding monsters of fascism were to share the loot, Mussolini had better start to show willing, somewhere soon.

Why Britain should have chosen to take on the Italians is not so clear. R. K. Webb in his book *Modern England*, seems to think that the popular reasons advanced for the decision – to keep Hitler from the oil-fields, to maintain allies . . . etc., was not the only thinking behind the North African war. He thought that it may have appealed to '. . . tradition, or recent memories: the ghost of the Gallipoli campaign, waged so disastrously at Churchill's insistence a quarter-century before, hovers strangely about British strategy.'

The British Army found the Italians easy meat and swept them from North Africa to Benghazi without much effort. In the beginning, however, they didn't do too well against the German Afrika Korps who had come to the aid of the Italians. Rommel very quickly threw the British back. The Germans were successful in Greece, too. The picture looked black indeed and it was only in the Near-East – in which Germany had no serious interest – that the British looked at all solid.

Meanwhile, back in the rest of the world, Germany attacked Russia on 22nd June, 1941; on 7th December, the Japanese attacked Pearl Harbor and Leo, who had rejoined the army in supplies, received his commission. Private Terence Alan Milligan, now the son of an officer and a gentleman, found a new girl-friend who had been a singer with the BBC, and she encouraged Spike to enter a music competition in the summer of the following year which, with the help of Lily Gibbs's trumpet, he won. Still at the seaside in Bexhill, Milligan's war was getting better and better.

Flo Milligan pleaded with the Virgin Mary to intercede with her Son in the war on behalf of her son, Terence, who was a Catholic like Himself, and that was how Bernard Montgomery from Ulster won game, set and match from General Erwin Rommel on 30th August, 1942.

The 'Desert Fox' retreated, having suffered heavy casualties at Cyernaica and Tripoli. Although Rommel escaped from the trap, Montgomery was already a winner when the Americans arrived on 7th November to begin combined operations. One

Irishman had succeeded in softening up the enemy for another. Spike Milligan arrived with 19 Battery, 56th Regiment, Royal Artillery, in North Africa on 3rd January, 1943.

Fourteen The Minstrel Boy

There never was a good war
or a bad peace.

Benjamin Franklin

Milligan's two and a half years at Bexhill-on-Sea had been the most rewarding of his life. It marked a hiatus: for two years he had been able to stand outside, as it were, and see himself in relation to his family, his condition and his class.

When he realized that he was a working-class youth the revelation must have come as a severe shock. In India he had not noticed the very poor. He saw how servants were treated and he came across beggars in the streets. But he had never realized, for example, that there were folk in Poona waiting on somebody to die that they might earn enough for a meal by carrying the corpse. Milligan had become poor in adolescence: and, because it was a condition to which he had not been reared, it was tough.

The army came as a godsend. He caught a glimpse of other meanings, and learned how to articulate his recently accepted convictions that man shouldn't have to work to live: that there are other values to be taken into consideration, such as the quality of life.

Since teaching is its own reward, it must have been fun for the scholars like Lieutenant Goldsmith or the other ex-university officers who had been roped in by Milligan to do a culture job on the lad from Catford. Spike was no Eliza Dolittle – his was a ready-made assimilative ego, one of countless millions which, for reasons of class, society had decided not to programme.

Goldsmith's translation of Flaubert's *L'Education Sentimentale* was published in 1941, and he had been correcting the proofs when he was called up in 1940. It would have been a good time to meet up with the raw, enquiring mind of his junior, Milligan. Like Flaubert and Elisa Schlessinger (the Marie Arnoux of *L'Education Sentimentale*), Spike had worn his heart on his sleeve for Lily Gibbs, and very publicly. However Spike tried to joke

Lily out of his emotions, Goldsmith would have understood the real state of Milligan's mind through Flaubert's feelings for Elisa:

> *He associated with people and he had other love affairs. But the memory of the first one made them indifferent to him. . . .*[1]

Flaubert seems to exercise a fascination for intellectuals of the wandering tribes, be they Jews, Irish or just plain Celtic. Thus, apart from Anthony Goldsmith's translation, there was J. M. Cohen who put Flaubert's letters into English, Gerard Hopkins translated *Madame Bovary*, and James Joyce unashamedly based his magnificent Molly Bloom on Emma Bovary herself. Maybe Milligan, Leopold Bloom, James Joyce and Gustave Flaubert all suffered all their lives the same pangs of jealousy that our lost tribes have endured since the Hibernians were barely Hebrew from Iberia. The fear of being cuckolded is always in the mind of the man who is not thinking of the insult to humanity but of the insult to himself. Thus in 1977 we find Milligan still tormenting himself with suspicions of infidelity:

> *In bed she said, 'I love you'*
> *To many another face.*
> *And once again each silver word*
> *Fell carefully into place.*[2]

We are told that 'sophisticated' men rationalize these fears and therefore suffer no pain in the infidelities of their wives and mistresses. It's much easier to appreciate the feelings of men like Milligan. Being educated and working class is a process of learning how to avoid vulgarity and eschew ignorance. 'Not a word of a lie' usually precedes some deliberate misrepresentation of fact; 'on my mother's life' predicts something at best apocryphal; and literary or historical attributions are frequently at best ascribed to the wrong originator.

The working class does not so much lie as invent reality. Knowledge or lack of knowledge is so often tied up with security of tenure of employment that, in order to prosper, many have become consummate liars. They think to gain by deceit what has been denied them by lack of education.

The working class is well versed in ignorance. Like Henry Ford's timekeeper who couldn't read the clock but needed the job, the sharpest ones lie in the hope that they will learn before it's too late. Milligan beat the odds because his working-class life in India was lived in middle-class circumstances; he had to fabricate little since, in the world of the Raj, only servants lie and cheat.

Richard Hoggart and Milligan fought the same war: a war in defence of an abstract humanity – but of their own people in particular. Men like Professor Haldane spoke about 'sharpening the class struggle', seeing it as seeing enemies on both sides. Hoggart, and Milligan in his own way, realized the limitations of their people, but familiarity bred an understanding of working-class foibles and failings. Milligan would never criticize his newly found family; Hoggart explains the working-class condition in a bid to improve their lot. At the same time, both of these intellectuals had started off in life a little more equal than many of their fellows.

Spike complained to me that in Catford he never had any birthday parties as a boy:

> *My mother never even had one birthday party for me as a child. Would you credit that?*

If we are to understand Milligan it is imperative that we know the nature of the cultural metamorphoses that took place between him enlisting at Bexhill-on-Sea in 1940 and arriving in North Africa in 1943. That his development and that of others like Hoggart are paralleled only goes to indicate the great awakening that was taking place now that millions of people were fighting together for a cause rather than quarrelling over the bones of some dusty archduke.

And that, more or less, was why young men from Britain and the Commonwealth found themselves on their way to North Afria in 1943. Spike remembered that it was a balmy night when the regiment landed after a terrible trip through the Bay of Biscay, during which German U-boats sank two of the outlying destroyers:

> *We arrived in the wonderful calm of the Mediterranean – it was a mill pond. It looked like a sea of milk with the moon shining on it.*

They had been forbidden prior to embarkation to take their instruments aboard, but they had brought them anyway:

> *The major came up and said, 'Look Milligan, there's a rumour*

going around that, despite orders to the contrary, you musician chaps brought your instruments with you, is that so?'

When Milligan admitted that the band was indeed equipped to make music, the CO asked if they would play at an officers' dance in the officers' mess aboard ship. Spike recalled that instead of punishment for disobeying orders, the same officer went round with the hat for the musicians:

And, when we came ashore, we played again because there were thousands of troops coming in with nothing to do. So they stuck us into an ENSA concert party. We brought the roof down playing jazz.

In those days he used to do an impression of Louis Armstrong.

Maybe I played a bit loud, but then that's why I wanted to play the trumpet in the first place. And yet, if they thought I played loud they should have heard our badgie I sometimes stood in for. Sergeant-Major Trumpeter Jumbo Jenkins blew himself a double rupture in a North African field. He was sounding the alarm call in five or six Gs which means immediate muster – not a sinner soldier moved.

Milligan's recollections of war are hardly those of the medalled memoirist – just as his history of war is not always a history of heroes and heroism. High in his priorities on arrival in North Africa was to make a pilgrimage to the many archaeological sites. Why archaeology should have attracted him so, Spike is at a loss to understand. He had not been interested in the study of human antiquities before enlisting in the army, he could swear to that. He doesn't even remember any discussion of the subject while at Bexhill:

It just happened when I arrived in North Africa: I was drawn to archaeology as if I'd been programmed for that sort of thing. You know there are some folk who believe that a person or animal is born with all the instructions already built in – it knows exactly what to do when it grows up. It's as if I had a built-in desire to be an archaeologist.

He made a habit of digging in all the ruins that they encountered wherever they fought. He suddenly realized that his war was being waged in the middle of Roman Africa.

> *All around me were these incredible examples of history. If only I'd had a box I could have collected shards, statues and God knows what – the Milligan marbles! At any rate I took time off from war and that's not a bad caper to take time off from.*

Winston Churchill and President Roosevelt discussed the North African campaign, code-named 'Operation Husky'. Churchill writes:

> *He [Roosevelt] suggested to me that it should be called 'Belly' and I advised 'Bellona'.*[3]

Spike doesn't refer to that discussion in any of his war books, but then he's not a real memoirist. He doesn't even remember the name of the place where he had his first real scare of the war; though he does remember what he was doing:

> *I was trying to get a telephone line up two trees near . . . what's this it was called? I forget the name of the hill. I didn't know that I was in full view of an enemy observation post. Suddenly this 88 mm gunner saw me and fired. . . .*

It burst behind him – such a low trajectory that he couldn't hear anything but a hissing noise:

> *Like a bloody fool – only an Irishman would go to inspect the damage – I started to walk over towards it to see what had happened. Then another one landed behind me and of course I ran like fuck down what's its-name hill. Two stars! Touch of England! The heroes! I'll tell you the odd thing about war, you inevitably run towards the flashpoints.*

As Spike was seeking any hole to creep into, a squadron of Stukka bombers were intent on blasting the London-Irish out of existence.

> *I thought that I was on my own, that the hole was empty but, when the smoke cleared, the place was simply full of these hairy Irishmen – big enormous warriors wearing kaili beards where they shaved just under the chin, and all their officers carried shillelaghs. Shillelaghs, for Christ's sake!*
> *They were all mad but I was glad they were on our side because just the thought of one of these fellows with a German accent would have made you run for your life. An Irish sergeant*

> *grabbed me by the arse and, hauling me to safety, said, 'Don't worry, lad, yeh'll be as safe as houses here with me.' Smoking a corn-cob pipe and puffing away, he reassured me with a smile. 'Sure had it not been for the war the likes of us would never have been able to afford the fare. Don't worry, boy, you couldn't be safer at home in your bed.'*

And yet neither bombs, bullets nor the tribulations of war could change the shy, sensitive nature of Milligan or turn him against humanity. He told me that throughout the whole of his life, he had come across only one man ready to admit to killing another human being. This was a Pole who said he never minded sticking his bayonet into 'a German's belly':

> *Most soldiers will never say it; will never admit to it. And yet somebody killed them – didn't they? And I must have played my part.*

One of Spike's duties as a signaller was to relay the word of command to the battery:

> *The officer would say, 'Fire!' and I'd shout down the phone, 'Fire!' and, at the end of that 'Fire!', somebody must have been killed.*

Did he think about things like that, then?

> *No. I was so annoyed with the enemy, you see. After all, had it not been for Hitler and his gang, I'd have been playing at St Cyprian's hall with my hair greased down in Brylcreem and with nothing more aggressive in mind than how to pull the bird with the biggest boobs. When I thought of St Cyprian's away out in North Africa it used to put me into a rage. Nothing aesthetic or even political about my war. At times like those it was totally personal.*

I thought he had been joking when he suggested that there was a school in surrendering at Sandhurst, but he repeated the accusation in bitter belief. Still, he was nonplussed at the reactions of some Germans whom his platoon had succeeded in taking prisoner:

> *We captured them at a place called Jabul Mahdi and, the way they came across the hill in their neatly pressed uniforms, you'd have thought that they were in charge of us. There was their officer in front of them, giving the lead-off word of command.*

He carried a white flag in which our sergeant blew his nose.
And that was only the beginning.

The platoon's job was to get the prisoners into some three-ton trucks that were parked precariously on a narrow mountain road; but the lead vehicle broke down and, while the perplexed captors stood kicking the tyres, the prisoner-of-war officer asked Milligan's CO if they were 'heffing trupple mit your engine?' Milligan's officer said, 'Yes, the bugger won't start!' 'Ehn vutt you like me to heff it mentit fur you?'

> *So here were we being reduced to idiots and our fellow says,*
> *'Would you really? How jolly sporting of you!' . . . Well, the*
> *superior Kraut turns to his men and orders, 'Hans, cummenzie*
> *here!' Hans gets to work on the lorry and, in no time, it's*
> *ticking over. The ober lieutenant turns, bows and says, 'All*
> *suitable for us to moof now.' Clicks his heels and reverses the*
> *whole thing – we were the losers, they the ones in charge.*

In March 1943, the Mediterranean theatre had changed so much in favour of the Allies that Churchill was expressing the hope that they would have ten British divisions in the First and Eighth Armies ready for a final push in the battle for the Tunisia tip.

Spike Milligan celebrated his twenty-fifth birthday when the Afrika Korps were routed at Tripoli on the 16th April.

Eight days later, during fierce fighting for 'Longstop Hill' near the village of Toukabeur, one of the last battles before the fall of Tunis, Lieutenant Anthony Goldsmith was killed. Churchill ended his commentary on the Allied victory in North Africa with the words, 'Personally, I am well satisfied with the way it has gone.' Spike Milligan was broken-hearted:

> *At Toukabeur*
> *The dawn lights stir,*
> *Whose blood today will spill?*
> *Today it's Tony Goldsmith's*
> *Seeping out on Longstop Hill* [4]

While Hamish Henderson remembered:

> *But dust blowing round them*
> *Has stopped up their ears*
>   *O for ever*
> *Not sleeping but dead.* [5]

Rather ridiculously, Milligan said, 'You know, Tony Gold-smith's death spoiled the war for me. It all got so serious after that.' In *Rommel? Gunner Who?* Spike tells us:

> *BSM MacArthur, almost mummified in dust, goes down the column. 'It's all over!' he's shouting – and it was. We camped at Oued Melah, told to 'stand alert for a call'. It never came. On 12th May the fighting ceased. The war in Tunis was over. 'Cup of tea?' said Edgington. 'Ah, cheers,' I said; 'let's tune into Radio Algiers.' We did.*[6]

Fifteen The D-day Dodgers

We're the D-day dodgers
out in Italy,
Always on the vino always on the spree,
Eighth Army scroungers and our tanks
We live in Rome among the Yanks,
The happy D-day dodgers of Sunny
Italy.

We landed at Salerno, a holiday with pay,
The Jerries sent the bands out to greet
us all the way,
We all joined hands, they gave us tea,
We all sang songs, the beer was free,
The happy D-day dodgers of Sunny Italy.

Hamish Henderson, *Songs of World War II*

Despite Lady Nancy Astor's poor opinion of the Eighth Army,
Spike Milligan's recollections of his arrival in Italy are not the
same as hers.

The regiment had been ordered from North Africa in September 1943 and, on the way from Setif to their port of embarkation,
Bizerta, they saw the result of the conflict of European fascism
fought out by the Allies and the Axis. Death, and devastation,
and the desert more a grave than ever. That was the legacy of
'Western' politics to the perplexed and patient peasants who
would shortly be known as inhabitants of a new phenomenon to
be called the 'Third World'.

To the vast majority of the defenders of democracy, these same
peasants seemed less important than the defeated Panzer divisions, military vanguard of gas chambers and strength through
euthanasia.

Although the people of this part of North Africa had been
civilized when Scipio came to dominate them in 146 BC and,
indeed, they had resisted the Greeks some five hundred years
before that, they were now just cluttering up the battlefield and
getting in the way of the war games.

Spike saw them as simple folk, whose land and livelihood had

108

been abused disgracefully by foreign aggressors who should have had the good manners to find some better way of sorting out the problems of civilization, or the decency to do their fighting in their own back yards. More military-minded mentors than Milligan considered the North Africans were ungrateful niggers who didn't even bother to turn out to cheer the departing liberators. Spike told me:

> *You couldn't believe that anybody could possibly survive such devastation; but young and old just stoically accepted that such desolation was an acceptable part of a poor person's life. They just buried another casualty and got on with it.*

Milligan had done a lot of growing since joining the Royal Artillery in 1940, but he actually grew up in the desert. Because war is the most hostile way to settle an argument, everything about conflict is incongruous. The same mortar that had blown a hole in scholarly Anthony Goldsmith's chest blew an ignorant bombardier to safety. Men in green and khaki uniforms killed each other for possession of 'Longstop Hill' and none of the indigenous Africans had ever heard of it – and none knows of it now. To the natives the desert is a place of peace where they can meditate on life.

That's what they say: the desert is a place to contemplate the present and dwell on the past. Its very vastness demands attention. Nor does all sand look the same – there are features, anonymous in pictures but which stand out in its physical presence. 'Most of the time,' said the old campaigners, 'the sand stayed put.' But the desert winds of summer brought the sand-storms to be followed by the storms wrapped in the cold winds of winter.

In 'Memory of North Africa' Milligan remembered the brightness of morning:

> Gone away is the morning
> its teasing light,
> The lit of the fire,
> the burn of its bright,
> The chill of the dawning
> the pass of the night . . .[1]

Milligan remembers the bombers: the gun teams stirring; the standing down; the first morning brew in the kerosene tin and the volley of guns. Most of all, what comes through Spike's written-down war thoughts is perplexity. Maybe it has to do with the nature of mirage: in the desert, a man's death did not only diminish his fellows, it puzzled them. Other war poets saw death in the same way. In *Return to Oasis*, an Australian soldier told how the first dead man he saw was one of his own. They were advancing, rifles at the port; he knew his name and number and that is something to know when a man's number is up.

> *'For the powers that be had made me check grade three.'* (*What sort of war was this? men actually killed*) . . . *He looked, and half expected the dead man to rise with no blood spilled and 'none intended'. The corpse would surely look at him and laugh and say, 'Fooled yeh there, sport!' But, when he looked again, he knew that there would be no resurrection for a headless torso lying under an unattached tin-hatted head on the desert sand.*[2]

As Spike and the 56th Regiment made their way towards Bizerta Harbour, it could hardly have seemed two years since General Richard O'Connor, after the Italian surrender to the Australians at Benghazi, had sent from Libya the following dispatch to London:

> *War Office intelligence summary, March 1941, other theatre. Detachments of the German Expeditionary Force under an obscure General, Rommel.*

The 'Desert Fox' was not to remain obscure for long. Having won back Tobruk from the 'Desert Rats', Erwin Rommel wore O'Connor's goggles on his own peaked cap until a day in 1944 when he swallowed two cyanide pills in Berlin.

But this was September 1943 and, ever since the beginning of May, the 56th Regiment, now massed with units of Alexander's Eighth Army, had been able to relax, for Tunis had been won on the 12th. And wasn't there the happy time with cocoa, brandy, tea and wine? For more than three months there had been celebrations and victory parades. It had been, in the words of Terence Alan Milligan, 'one almighty binge'.

And then Spike suffered his first attack of 'battle fatigue'. Just before the fall of Tunis, his battery had lost men when one of their own shells prematurely exploded. Spike lived a 'nocturnal hell' of nightmare and hallucination for months afterwards:

*I just couldn't get the awful carnage out of my mind, you see,
and even when my old comrades hold a reunion to recall the
victory parades through Tunis, all I ever see are the faces of
my dead friends.*

A man is hit and rolls upon his back wearily to die. In the quiet
of such an uneasy peace Milligan tried to live all his life in daylight.

To get away as far as possible from himself, Spike organized
concert parties, and visits to places of interest. Especially he
wanted to see the archaeological sites at Carthage. It was along
this very Tunis-to-Bizerta road that he and his friends had set
out in the early summer to look at history but, above all, to hold
a picnic on the way.

Milligan loves picnics and all that reminds him of children
and childhood with his father in India – open-air sandwiches
and 'shooting the buck'. It's as if doing now what he and Leo
did before will make everything all right. Let the past free him
from the present: no now without then:

*There was no moon, but the sky was a pin-cushion of stars.
Great swathes of astral light blinked at us across space. We
made a fire, glowing scarlet in cobalt-black darkness, showers
of popping sparks jettisoning into the night air. Tins of
steak-and-kidney pud were in boiling water, with small bubbles
rising to the surface.*[3]

The concert parties were such a great success that a full variety
show to be called *Stand Easy* was put into rehearsal. But, before
it could take to the boards, the orders which were now taking the
56th Regiment to HMS *Boxer* had come through, and that was
why they were on their way to Salerno.

On 22nd September, 1943, Spike and his trumpet and his regiment left North Africa for the Italian front. They didn't, he
says, arrive in Italy either as conquerors or liberators: 'We landed
with Germans shooting at us – that's how we came.' It was D-
day plus fourteen at Salerno and he remembers that the shit was
all over the place when they ran like hell for cover. It wasn't
easy.

Then he went up the mountains and he remembers going in
a bren carrier in the middle of the night to an observation
post:

> *There was great mortaring going on ahead and the road was blocked and there was flames and bullets and bombs that lit up the night sky so that you could have read a newspaper with no trouble. No, we didn't go there as conquerors, we arrived in Italy shit-scared and that is the truth.*

It was December and the most popular song with the Eighth Army was the 'D-day Dodgers', written by the finest of World War II poets, Captain Hamish Henderson. They sang it to the tune of 'Lily Marlene' and they invited Lady Astor to:

> *Look across the mountains*
> *In the wind and rain,*
>   *See the wooden crosses,*
> *Some that bear no name.*
> *Heart-break and toil*
> *And suffering gone,*
>   *The lads beneath them*
> *Slumber on,*
>   *The lucky D-day dodgers*
> *Who'll stay in Italy.*[4]

Milligan got sand-fly fever and was hospitalized. After a while he rejoined the regiment at Volturno, and they fought their way right through the mountains up to the Carigliano:

> *We did have some magic moments. We spent one night that I shall never forget as long as I live, in a little place on the Divine Coast, Amalfi. It was a place people only read about before the war, where artists and important people used to stay.*
>   *They still do, in fact. Gore Vidal lives there now. He's part Irish; did you know that?*

I didn't but I do now:

> *That's where the name 'Gore' comes from. Remember Yeats's poem 'In Memory of Con and Eva Gore-Booth', the two sisters about whom he wrote:*
>
> > *Two girls in silk kimonos, both*
> > *Beautiful, one a gazelle?*
>
> *Beautiful poetry. Do you know that the first poetry I ever purchased was Virgil's 'Aeneid'. You know why I bought it? It looked very nice – very attractive, beautifully printed.*

He and his comrades were enraptured by the 'Divine Coast', by the friendliness of the people, by the fisher-folk singing. Spike loves to recall that in those days there were no tourists, no discos. To his surprise he met there, amongst all those Italian villagers, a Cockney woman all in black, waving and inviting them up for a meal and a drink:

> Her place overlooked the 'Divine Coast' – as it was called in those parts. And it was a lustrous moonlit night – a crescent moon that looked for all the world like a toenail hanging from the sky. Down below was the sound of the piscatories out fishing all night. They had little lamps in the prows of their ships and they looked minuscule on this great sea which was reflected like tinted silver paper.

The fishermen were singing and beating on the prow of their boats with the rollocks:

> And do you know that all that beating and singing was to attract the fish? Dad used to warn me to keep very still and silent when he went fishing in the Nilgari Hills back in India and here were these piscatories kicking up bloody murder – of course, then they were trying to catch Italian fish so a few operatic arias would probably have been as good a temptation as anything else.

Then this Cockney lady gave them a wonderful dinner: 'spaghetti, wine and God knows what':

> Ken Carter, who started Benny Hill off in the early TV days, played some of his own compositions. I think Harry Secombe sang, and Edgington played his piano as we sat on this balcony and enjoyed this divine night. The tranquillity has never left me in my life . . . Then we had to get back to the bloody war.

Christmas Day, 1943, saw the regiment in barracks near Naples. They were, as was army custom, served dinner by their officers and, in the evening, the 19th battery put on a concert with Spike as the trumpet-playing MC. The concert ran for hours and was a great success. Spike was now quite convinced that what he wanted to be more than anything else was a professional entertainer, and that, as he's fond of saying, was at least a start.

The new year brought with it a fiercer resistance from the retreating German Army, and at Lauro, on the advance towards

Cassino, the British suffered many casualties. They went up to Lauro on a dark night round about the first of January. Milligan remembered the night in his poem, 'The Soldiers at Lauro':

> Young are the dead
> Like babies they lie
> The women they blest once
> Not healed dry
> And yet – too soon
> Into each space
> A cold earth falls
> On colder face
> Quite still they lie
> These fresh reeds
> Clutched in earth
> Like winter seeds
> But these will not bloom
> When called by spring
> To burst with leaf
> and blossoming
> They will sleep on
> In silent dust
> As crosses rot
> And memories rust.[5]

'Happy New Year' they were all saying as they dug into a mountain of mud. Milligan never saw such 'Happy New Years' in all his life. Shot, bombs, bullets – the terrifying shit of war:

> Yes, I was terrified – everybody was. Everybody was scared stiff, but what could you do? Nothing you can do when you've been run over by a bus! You have to accept it. That was it – you were run over by a bloody bus.

Milligan's attempts to understand war have the sense of desperation. When was it ever necessary? When did any conflict achieve anything?

> Apart from the last effort against fascism. That had to be defeated – didn't it? We didn't think, I suppose. The comradeship was wonderful. I came, you see, from a mixed regiment, some London boys and a throw-in of Liverpudlians or Irish – that is the same thing.

On 22nd January, 1944, Milligan was wounded in the left leg and badly shaken as he lay unattended with shells falling all around him. He was eventually picked up by one of his mates, Bob (Dipper) Dye, and carried to the nearest first-aid post. A nervous major in a state of panic abused the injured Milligan for being a malingerer and Spike still trembles with rage as he remembers the occasion:

> *Until I was blown up at Lauro, I could have slept on bricks. In fact I used to doze off by the 7.2 mm howitzers while they were going off. So, when this stupid supercilious major abused me, for a moment I thought: Now that I'm taken out of the line and down-graded from Bombardier, I'm guilty of being a coward. Then, on reflection, I remembered that I'd been in action for more than a year and a half! If I was going to run away, I'd have run away before now!*

Milligan spends a lifetime of agonizing self-analysis during which torture there is nobody harder on him than himself. He figures that he was the victim of an anxiety complex – he went back into the line too quickly. He believes that the British weren't prepared for shell-shock cases, and that was the trouble. The yanks had it all figured out as 'battle fatigue'.

Although the Allies had been in the military ascendancy for more than two years, politicians in Whitehall and the Pentagon nearly gave the war to the Axis. The Eighth Army in Italy, fighting to support an Allied invasion behind German lines at Anzio, almost came to grief. The politicians in London and Washington couldn't make up their minds if a win for the Italian partisans was the sort of victory they were seeking. Fortunately, the partisans were in virtual control of Rome and the best part of Italy. The Germans, therefore, with their hands full, were in no position to inflict the defeat on the Allies that the false strategy at Anzio had invited.

Spike had all but broken down, mentally and physically. What with battle fatigue and piles – 'the most debilitating illness from which a fighting man can suffer' – he could say goodbye to service in the line, much as he begged to be allowed to rejoin his comrades in 'D' battery.

If there ever was a good time for fighting this was hardly it. For nearly three years – since the German invasion of Russia on 22nd June, 1941 – Europe had been calling for the opening of a second front. Now the call could be resisted no longer; and after some more delays and more bickering about political strategy, the Second Front was launched in Europe – the main thrust coming in Normandy on 6th June, 1944:

> *It's here, chum, it's here, chum*
> *The Second Front for you,*
> *In spite of the old Atlantic Wall,*
> *And the boys to see it through,*
> *It won't take long to finish it,*
> *Once we have got their range,*
> *And then we can all go home*
> *And live like humans for a change.*[6]

Sixteen Goodbye to All That

I had no fears now
about dying. I was content
to be wounded and on the way home.

Robert Graves, *Goodbye to All That*

Since January, Spike had been in rehabilitation at Afrigola and Banio, before being transferred to an officers' rest camp just south of Naples. He became a wine waiter in the officers' dining-room and occasionally played the piano, either to pass the time, or at the request of his superiors.

Milligan had, after the outburst of the panic-stricken major at Lauro, been demoted, and it was with some pleasure he learned that he was to be made up again to Bombardier. This promotion came about after he was appointed driver to Major Tony Clark, who put his hand up Spike's shorts and got thumped for the liberty.

In *Where Have All the Bullets Gone?* Major Clark appears as Colonel Stanley, and Milligan describes how in 1970 he died from piles and not, as everybody had suspected, from alcoholic poisoning of his liver or bladder:

> *But for piles, Stanley would be alive today, doing ten years for interfering with little boys. One of them could have been me. I speak with experience. You see, that evening on our return from Ischia I drove Stanley back to his billet and he put his hand up my shorts. I thought, this could mean promotion for me, but no, I said, 'Look here, sir . . . fuck off.' He is sorry. It will never happen again. Len falls about laughing, 'Cor, fancy, there's men up the line dying and down here the colonels are trying to grab yer goolies.' I reminded him it was better than dying. 'Let's face it, would you rather be fucked or killed?'* [1]

Recycled actuality is all grist to the Milligan. Thus, in *Puckoon*, Uncle Willie is resurrected in the persona of Mr Pearce, whose very name itself is a play on that of Patrick Henry Pearse, the Nationalist leader in the Easter Rising. Despite Milligan's dedicated patriotism, he rejects any form of jingoism. There is no way that he would ever contribute to a personality cult, even when the personality concerned is dead.

P. H. Pearse is seen in Ireland as a charismatic figure – tall, tough, gentle and saintly. Spike's character is 'Little Mr Pearce . . . a parchment-dry face locked under a flat cap . . . heavy pebble glasses giving him the appearance of a goitrous elf.' And he boasts, 'In all the fighting the English never caught me.' They had never known about the grenades hidden in his hollow leg.

Spike is afraid of cults and, while satirizing his own, he reserves proper respect for the proper occasion. He celebrates the 'Rising' and honours the leaders of '16' well:

> *The lights had gone out!*
> *The sun cannot set!*
> *The green heart is suppurating!*
> *Heroes' souls are on the English rack*
> *And the harp's strings are muted.*
>
> *In the fusillade*
> *a child is born in blood*
> *his heritage will be glory.*
>
> *Goodnight Padraig Pearse*
> *and your friends.*[2]

Yeats, as we know, also wrote a memorable 'Easter 1916', but Spike saw it in his own inimitable way. He didn't have any axe to grind with the women of the men involved, so he didn't have to dwell on anything but the deed.

And so, it's not on sealing-wax, cabbages and kings or anything so mind-worthy that The Milligan meditates in *Puckoon*, but heroes with cowards' legs, and captains stroking 'cavalry moustaches' on infantry faces. When one man retreats, complains The Milligan, it's called running away:

> '*But a whole regiment running away is called a retreat? I demand to be tried by cowards.*'
> *A light, commissioned-ranks-only laugh passed around the court. But this was no laughing matter. These lunatics could have him shot.*[3]

Thus, from the first joke he told Anthony Goldsmith, Milligan had been developing the style he presently perfected. Ideas now come one after the other in goonlike juxtaposition, the effect being to present on the printed page the cleverly illogical 'lateral' thinking of The Milligan, who is also bringing only half his own thinking into conscious focus:

> *I like to get the idea across quickly, briefly. I couldn't write anything like* Childe Harolde *which goes on for about forty pages and bores the arse off everybody.*

During his time as clerk-driver at Maddaloni, Naples, Spike was far from well. Despite endless, sometimes senseless notes to his Battery Commandant begging to be returned to 19th Battery, he was kept at Second Echelon for a period of recuperation and was assigned only light duties. He began playing his trumpet again and, from contacts he had made as piano-playing wine waiter at Portici Officers' Club, he was soon back making music on a grand scale.

There were two thousand officers and men at 'Mad' Maddaloni barracks, many of them mentally disturbed and mostly from the war. In the forties it was common to ignore such patients, and quite frequently sensible treatment, such as work and art therapy, was tried only by an enlightened few. This can be particularly disturbing in the case of people like Milligan who depend for inspiration on a shared muse. All Spike's life has been lived needing people. He has, you see, the grand design always in mind; he thinks that art creation can be shared – no mystery to it: musicians play, writers write, sculptors sculpt and painters paint. What could be simpler than an artists' co-operative?

Van Gogh felt like that and it destroyed him. He couldn't begin to understand why Gauguin, Toulouse-Lautrec, Bernard and Aquetin didn't want to come and make art with him at the 'Yellow House'. To Van Gogh that reaction was incredible, and so homesickness and loneliness drove him to suicide at the age of thirty-seven. This wasn't going to happen to Milligan, for he learned how to accept the schizoid side of his introversion and call up his other self – or dismiss him as the need arose:

> *Someone left the mirror running*
> *I pulled the plug out*
> *It emptied my face*
> *and drowned my reflection.*

> *I tried mouth to mouth*
> *resuscitation*
>
> *the glass broke*
> *my reflection died*
> *Now there's only one of me.*[4]

Just as cunningly, Spike makes his neuroses work for him. Psychiatrists say that the symptomatology of the manic is characterized by exaltation and excitement, loquaciousness and rapid association of ideas. Spike feels that in times of depression the thing to do is to write – principally poetry, but writing of any sort will work therapeutically. Above all, making music works for him and gives him a great feeling of well-being.

Recently he told me that today he is manic depressive: 'It's as if you're on the floor. You don't have any legs. Despairing is the word. Churchill suffered a lot from manic depression – he called it 'The Black Dog'. Winston's depressions were never like Spike's; nobody's were:

> *All people have depressions, but mine are manic. They – I*
> *don't know what 'they' means really – are, as it were,*
> *magnified. Like through a microscope. There's no feeling of*
> *pain – there's no actual feeling. It's abstract. It's like looking*
> *at a glass of water and asking people to say if it's hot or cold.*
> *It's just impossible.*

It is likely that Milligan, in 1944, was suffering from schizophrenia. He exhibited many of the symptoms, such as thought-disorder and hesitancy of speech. The symptoms noted by Spike nowadays are hardly consonant with manic depressiveness. For that again, the tears he shed when he realized that Major Tony Clark's interest in him as a driver was not completely altruistic are quite in keeping with the pre-psychotic state of the manic depressive – lability, mood swings, and unpredictable oscillations of emotion. Could it be that doctors have not as yet managed to identify genius in its conceptual state?

In the meantime, enlightened psychiatrist-therapists gave Milligan and some other patients the job of decorating the bar of the officers' mess at Maddaloni barracks. A former newspaper cartoonist, Lieutenant Robb, drew some sketches and Spike painted the murals. For a while Milligan also played with the O2E dance orchestra until an unusually strict doctor said Spike had a weak chest and mustn't play the trumpet any more.

Poor Milligan. In those days it seldom rained but it poured. And yet there is something decidedly odd about the way he accepted that diagnosis in 1944. Spike has seldom taken anybody's advice or verdict unless it has suited him to do so.

Without complaint he submitted to the will of his army GP and stopped blowing the horn, never to pick it up again – until the occasion demanded. Had he been waiting subconsciously for some excuse to leave music aside for a while so as to involve himself in some other of the creative arts? Since Milligan seldom lets the left side of his mind know how the right side is thinking, we may never know.

Meanwhile Lieutenant Robb had encouraged the patients in the building of an 'other ranks' club – an idea generated by Milligan who had informed Lieutenant Robb that private soldiers had little to do in the way of relaxing therapeutically.

On a more official level, Combined Services Entertainments had presented West End plays that encouraged Milligan to giggle – much to the consternation of soap fans. Spike decided to parody this popular light-weight theatre and didn't know that the genre into which he had dipped his pen was called satire. The journal of the officers of the Second Echelon, *The Valjean Times*, noticed Spike's *Men in Gitis* on 22nd March, 1944:

> *The high spot was undoubtedly,* Men in Gitis, *a satirical sequel to* Men in Shadows. *This type of show is either liked or hated, and quite a few did not care for it at all, but the majority of people present gave the distinguished performers a really good ovation. Spike Milligan was at his craziest, and the show was a cross between* Itma *and* Hellzapoppin.[5]

Inevitably Spike got himself seriously disliked by the 'Leather Suitcase' brigade. And small wonder. He insisted on writing scripts which, in his own words, 'sent them up rotten'. It was no great surprise when in July 1945, the sensitive souls in command posted Bombardier Milligan to the Central Pool of Artistes. 'There,' said Brigadier Wood of Maddaloni, 'he could make fun of the whole of the Imperial General Staff and blow his trumpet as loud as he wished.' The first production he appeared in was a variety show called *Over the Page* in which Harry Secombe was the leading comic.

Although he had heard Harry sing that night at Amalfi, Milligan insists that this was his first meeting with the Welsh artist. In *Rommel? Gunner Who?* Spike says, 'It appears memories always have to be forced on us,' and maybe he's right for, in the same book, Milligan states quite categorically that he and Harry met a year earlier:

> It was about this time that I saw something that I felt might put years on the war. It was a short gunner, wearing iron-frame spectacles, a steel helmet that obscured the top of his head, and baggy shorts that looked like a Tea Clipper under full sail. He was walking along a gulley behind a group of officers, heaped with equipment. It was my first sight of Gunner Secombe. . . . I never dreamed one day he, I, and a lone RAF clerk called Sellers, at that moment in Ceylon imagining he could hear tigers, would make a sort of comic history.[6]

Secombe, like Milligan, had been posted to the CPA because he was suffering from nervous exhaustion brought on by battle fatigue. Whether they had met before or not is a moot point; from now on they very quickly became firm friends and did a few ad lib shows together while waiting for *Over the Page* to go into production. But Spike noticed that, however well their act went down, Secombe wanted to make it very much on his own. This, though, was a forgivable foible in the make-up of a man renowned for his generosity of spirit.

Milligan remembers only the best in his friends; life is much too short to recall the transient unpleasant. He says that the funniest time he had with Secombe was after the war when they were all very poor, although Harry had enough to buy beans and toast for a gang of mendicant thespians at the local Lyons Corner House in London. They were sitting at a table in the Lyons café, eating their toast and beans, when Secombe pulled his raincoat over his head and buttoned it up in imitation of Brendan Behan doing his impersonation of Synge's old woman of the world bewailing her woes, which he had seen Behan do at the Garrick Club bar. Harry's face was so well hidden that he couldn't see anything outside, so Milligan and company rose silently and crept out of the restaurant. They stood on the pavement looking through the window until a huge crowd had gathered behind them. Milligan laughs:

*He went on doing his act for a good ten minutes – doing the
whole thing to nobody! And when we told him, he just laughed
uproariously. I wonder, would he still react in the same way?
Oh, I'm sure he would.*

Although Spike talks about the day they first met, I think he
really means when he and Harry came to work with the CPA:

*The day we first met I can recall very clearly. I had gone to
hospital because the war had made me a bit crazy. I was
discharged because this Brigadier Wood didn't like me
playing my trumpet so loud. We were both posted to the Central
Pool of Artistes at about the same time. Secombe sang and I
played any instruments I could lay my hands on, but mainly
trumpet and piano.*

And yet, if Harry knew where he was going, so did Spike.
Milligan might not appear to be as single-minded, but life is
something he has got used to over the years; he can take it by the
scruff of the neck and mould it in his image whenever the need
arises. The eccentric Milligan is more illusion than reality. Any
man who can suddenly arrange, in the middle of an air-raid, to
play bootleg music on bootleg instruments, will have few problems finding his way around the world of entertainment.

The time in Italy until Spike's discharge from the army in
October 1946 was crammed with the business of show business.
He and the 'Bill Hall Trio' eventually became the hit of *Over the
Page*. For a year they had toured Italy in the style to which only
finishing school-leavers were accustomed. In Trieste he had met
up with and nearly married the singer Antoinette Pontani who
became the central character in his novel, *Goodbye Soldier*.

He didn't want to leave Italy. Above all, he hated the idea of
breaking up the trio: they were big-time and continental; Catford
and Lewisham would never be the same as Rome, Naples and
Trieste. Lily Gibbs was married and his mother would never
take the place of Toni:

*The CSE was a life-line. I was mixing with artists who were
all soldiers. There was Harry and Bill and Norman Vaughan
. . . and God knows everybody passed through there at some
time. No shortage of food, and pretty girls all over the place.
The Yanks could think what they liked . . . we were the Allies!*

Imagine me and Lily trying to make up the price of the cinema in Catford and here was I with free seats for the San Carlo Opera House – me and Toni Pontani: God I loved that girl for a while!

Certainly Milligan's goodbye to Italy in '46 was a much more reluctant one than that of the 56th Highland Division's departure eighteen months earlier:

> *Farewell ye dives o' Sicily,*
> *Fare ye well yer shilen's an' ha's,*
> *We'll a' mind shebeens and bothys*
> *Whaur kind signorinas were cheery*
>
> *Farewell ye banks o' Sicily,*
> *Fare ye well yer valleys and shores*
> *There's no' a Jock will mourn the*
> *   kyles o' ye*
> *Poor bloodie swaddies are weary.*[7]

Seventeen On the Road

I'm goin' down the road
feelin' sad,
I'm goin' down the road
feelin' sad,
I'm goin' down the road feelin'
sad, Lord, Lord,
An' I ain't gonna be treated
this a-way.

Woody Guthrie, 'Bound for Glory'

While Spike Milligan was getting himself ready for the peace, the British people made it clear that peacetime was no time for old warriors like the wartime Prime Minister. On 18th May, 1945, Mr Churchill proposed that the coalition government continue until Japan was defeated. The Labour Party refused, and Winston insisted on an immediate general election. On 5th July, Labour was returned with a sweeping majority. The old bear went to the opposition benches while the ship of state was to be skippered by Clement Attlee, endearingly thought of by Winston as 'a sheep in sheep's clothing'.

A year later, rationing and shortages were still the order of the day when Spike Milligan arrived back in England. Theatre hadn't changed a great deal yet, and it must have seemed, as he made his way from Victoria Station, that every playhouse in London was either playing something by Noël Coward or directed by him: he had even taken over British cinema. No doubt Noël was being justly rewarded for courage beyond the call. With little thought of the risks involved he had mixed with the lower orders, after which sacrifice he was now back with his own in the West End. At the time it never struck Milligan that it was this very 'Coward Codology' that he had made fun of in *Men in Gitis*, and to which blasphemy the defenders of the inconsequential had taken grave exception.

In order to send Desmond to Reigate School of Art and move his family from Catford, Leo had sold his pension back to the army. It was, therefore, to a rented terraced house, 3, Leathwell

Road, Deptford, that Spike was bound on a day in November when cold smog was still the London weather.

It wasn't the same as Naples; there wasn't the sun or the hope. But optimism can make up for a lot and, while Milligan may frequently be down, he is seldom out. Since leaving Bill Hall at Victoria, he had been going over in his mind the stories he would have to tell, and thinking of the tales he would hear from his father. Desmond was a big boy now and Flo would be changed. Spike told himself that he would understand things much better now and his mother would know him and appreciate his needs. Before joining up he hadn't realized that we are all of us perfect unto ourselves but seldom perfect to each other. Things would now, he felt, be different: after all the world had been through in the past six years people would be more mindful of each other's needs; that was bound to be the case, for the war had changed everything.

In a state of high excitement Spike made his way up the garden path, only to find that Flo, Leo and Desmond were away for the weekend, and the only one to welcome Spike was a begrudging neighbour who told him that if he didn't stop peering through the windows of the Milligan household she would send for the police. 'Some homecoming,' said Milligan, 'some bloody home.' In her last letter to him as a soldier his mother had been so solicitous:

> *Mother harps on about not forgetting to go to church. She thanks me for the photo of Toni that I sent her, but feels she would rather have had a medical report. Don't forget to put paper on the toilet seat. If I can't, do it standing up.*

Remembrance still makes him angry:

> *Put paper on the seat! After six years there was nobody there even to open the bloody door!*

When Flo realized that the war had 'taught her eldest boy nothing' about important things like work and Mass, she despaired of him ever being able to make his way in the real world. It was all very unfair: she had not begrudged her son, and all that she had asked in return was that the army might make a Christian man of him. The country had let her down: none of his faults had been remedied, no flaw put right. Flo was convinced that the war had only succeeded in changing his character

126

for the worse – it had taken a boy with an interest in music and sent back a bohemian; and God knew there was not a great call for that type in the East End of London.

And, if all that wasn't worrying enough, he had brought back his own bad company. When she first met Johnny Mulgrew and Bill Hall, Flo could hardly believe that such unkempt individuals would be admitted to a respectable theatre, let alone play in one. They wouldn't have been in her day! Besides which, she decided that the leader of the Bill Hall Trio was a drunk. Flo never knew, but the Bill Hall Trio had been hot stuff from Naples to Capri.

And so, on this cold day in November 1946, Spike climbed through a window and found that the new house was not unlike the old one – inside, indeed, it looked much the same. It was as if they had moved Riseldine Road to a different area, and added a bathroom. As Milligan looked around the house he found copies of the same newspapers that this mother had sent to him in Italy. He remembered the headlines in *Goodbye Soldier*: 'Bread Ration; No Change Yet'; 'Heath for Trial on Chine Murder Charge'. A caption on the *Daily Herald* read, 'Mr Attlee Says Prisons are Overcrowded'.

When the family reunited, it was as though he had never left. It seemed to Milligan that in his absence Flo had become even more bitter about how he was growing up.

> *Christ! I'd been through a bloody war and she didn't even treat me like a school-leaver.*

As Leo tried to keep the peace, Spike and his mother waged war. It was obvious to him now that she would never accept the life he had chosen for himself. It was no longer a question of would he fly the coop, but when.

When? Aye, there's the rub. Nobody but Irishmen or musicians would have picked the winter of 1946/47 to take a new group on the road, but the Bill Hall Trio needed money and Spike Milligan needed peace.

It was the worst winter on record. People were skating on the Thames and wearing overcoats in the House of Commons. MP Phil Piratin said that God had joined the Tory Party and, how-ever far-fetched that possibility might seem, it was clear that Heaven wasn't doing Labour any favours. Emanuel Shinwell, as minister responsible, couldn't have picked a worse year to put the nationalization of fuel and power onto the statute books. Bertrand Russell thought that, because of poor stewardship, the former owners of mines and transport should not have been compensated, while Willie Gallagher, MP for West Fife, thought that they should have been jailed. On the whole, Spike Milligan worried that, because of a coal shortage, the central heating systems were not working and the theatres were freezing and empty.

But the Bill Hall Trio persisted; for they were bound by the same motto that has starved quite a few performers to death: 'The show must go on.' Bill Hall was a tall Irishman who played the best violin on the jazz scene – most of the others were what they called fiddle players, but Bill was a real violinist, the Grapelli of his day. Spike played the guitar and Johnny Mulgrew the double-bass. The truth is that, according to Spike, there was little else any of them could do: Johnny Mulgrew didn't know any other job, Bill Hall wouldn't have been employed in any other job, and Spike Milligan would have died rather than give Flo the satisfaction of seeing him do any other job.

The trio didn't make a lot of money, but what with private parties and the occasional theatre and club appearance, they avoided having to 'rest' through the notorious winter. And this, believe it or not, when the weather had destroyed the football league programme, closed hundreds of factories and brought much transport to a standstill, was an achievement.

In January 1947, they made their first television appearance and failed to impress the impresario Val Parnell. Apart from that and a few provincial dates, nothing much happened that year until, in July, Grandmother Kettleband dropped in from Poona, and Spike in a suit acted as best man for his brother when Desmond in uniform married Kathleen Roberts at Lewisham Catholic chapel in August; while in Grandma Kettleband's absence, the Labour Government gave India to the Indians in the same week.

Still there was one small victory for Flo. At least one of her children obeyed Mother Church without question and attended to his religious duties; with Leo as a fellow traveller of the Pope, it was as much as she was going to get, however high her expectations.

It wasn't that Spike set out to reject the teachings of the church or go the opposite way to his mother for pure cussedness: Milligan had other things on his mind. The Bill Hall Trio was a great act – they were musically brilliant and they did very funny comic routines. But they were all Indians and no chief. Their behaviour was totally anarchic and everybody knows that anarchists can organize little unless there is a leadership to oppose. Really they needed an agent.

At about the same time, somebody else was looking for representation. Peter Sellers' mother, Peg, wanted somebody to manage her son. He was a young up-and-coming trooper and she knew he was going to be 'just brilliant'. Peg should know? Who should know better? She was Jewish and theatrical – one such advantage would be enough for most people.

Yet few folk wanted to trust her judgement. 'Peg,' they told her, 'your son is a nice boy ... a nice Jewish boy ... but as an actor he's a *schlemiel* ... he stinks.' They all wanted to be Peg's agent because they knew that she was the one with the talent. Besides which, Peter's old man had been a Protestant and the boy himself had been educated at Highgate Catholic School – who ever learned how to chant 'Kol Nidre' in a chapel choir?

No, better the mother than the boy; but, what the hell, first things first: maybe the way to the mother is through the boy.

Denis Selinger didn't want to sign Peter Sellers. He did it originally to placate Peg and, years later, he admitted as much to Sellers' biographer, Peter Evans:

> In fact I was more impressed with Peg than with Pete at the first meeting.[1]

Sellers' mother sold the agent on the great comic actor:

> 'You are,' said Peg seriously, 'a very fortunate young man, Mr Selinger. My son is going to be worth a lot of money in this business one day. Listen to an old woman who knows.'[2]

Two rare theatre-woman, Flo Milligan and Peg Sellers. But while one thought that proficiency at acting was a gift from God, to the other it was the hallmark of an ill-spent youth.

Milligan told me that the Sellers, mother and son, loved each other. Peter would kiss her like a lover, 'Most unhealthy'. Wherever he was in the world Sellers would always ring home, and he would never take any important step without acquainting Peg. Milligan had to hide everything from his mother: the bottle parties, the clubs, the theatre work, the small successes; Flo believed that show business was the work of the devil.

At that time Sellers had just been sacked as entertainments manager of a Jersey holiday camp, the company having decided that Peter wasn't the stuff from which real redcoats are made. Milligan had come across Harry Secombe and Norman Vaughan again; they were living in a bed-sitter in Notting Hill Gate.

Vaughan and Secombe shared a room that Secombe had reduced to a state of chaos, so untidy was he. Milligan had been aware of Harry's habits for some time; in *Where Have All the Bullets Gone?* he describes Secombe's return to the CPA:

> *Secombe has been cured and released, and the hospital burnt down for safety. 'Hello hello, hey hoi hup.' He revolves round the hotel at speed. What had eluded scientists for 2000 years has been discovered by Gunner Secombe. Perpetual motion.*[3]

Spike says that Harry didn't try to be untidy or break things – he didn't have to. It would, of course, be a change for Spike, so used to his mother's house where there was a place for everything and everything in its place. This liberty hall he dearly wanted to enter.

And yet, he didn't feel like sharing with anybody, so he rented a room on his own. To Norman and Harry, the luxury of living alone was quite intemperate; however, they knew that Milligan was a very private person, despite his extrovert public persona. Spike set himself a release date from his mother, effective immediately. He resolved to place Flo on his mailing list, along with Toni Pontani and the inevitable Lily Gibbs (now a widow and due to appear in Milligan's books under her real name, Dunford). In the spring of 1947 he moved into 13, Linden Gardens, Notting Hill Gate.

The trio were becoming well known. They had played a tour which included a week at the Prince's Theatre, Blackpool and at the Glasgow Pavilion; after which they appeared in the usual 'out of town' venues from Manchester to Liverpool. But, when Spike came to live in Notting Hill, Harry Secombe assured him that he would get nowhere in show business without the help of an agent. Harry, a time-served theatrical, was doing well himself, but his feet were always securely on the ground. Generous to a fault, although he didn't spend money unnecessarily, he was always a great believer in Milligan's genius and tolerant of his frequent petulant outbursts. It was Secombe who arranged for Spike and Norman Vaughan to audition for the part of resident comedian at the Windmill Theatre, and Spike told me:

*I had never thought of the Van Dams as running anything
more than a high-class strip-tease show. It wasn't even as good
as the ones in the Soho Cellars, since the Windmill girls weren't
even permitted to move.*

Spike's audition came to grief when he walked on the stage
with the words, 'Sorry I came on fully dressed.' The Van Dams
didn't see the humour of the remark and simply called for the
'next please'. Spike took the dismissal in seething silence, feign-
ing, as he often did, a philosophical disregard, but Norman was
indignant:

*Shows how short-sighted they were. It wasn't a bad beginning.
They could have listened for a few minutes. Bastards, weren't
they?*[4]

However, for a while it seemed that with the coming of autumn
1947, things were going to change for the better. Spike had kept
on his room at Notting Hill Gate and, when the trio came back
from Scotland, they found a fistful of dates waiting.

They did some successful shows in London and were immediately signed up for a European tour. They went to Zurich
and on to Rome where Spike met Toni Pontani again, only to
realize that they were no longer compatible. Toni had given up
show business and joined the ranks of the Flo Kettlebands. Show
business she decided was not the career for her future husband,
and certainly not with Bill Hall and Johnny Mulgrew.

Spike blames himself, as he always does, for the vagaries of
women, but really he was just not ready to settle down. He had
some youth to get back which had been stolen from him by the
war. He knew that there was no future with the trio, but only
because he was moving away from that field of entertainment.
The army and things like *Men in Gitis* at that time, he now
realized, were merely a gestation period. He now knew what he
had been doing when he satirized the West End soap.

He left Toni in Rome and the trio went on to play in Milan,
Verona, Savona, Trieste and Bergamo. Near Yugoslavia they
joined the Italian Communist Party because this was the only
way they could get a meal. They swore vengeance on the capitalist class and in particular theatrical agents who welshed on agree-
ments.

A visit to the British Embassy in Rome did little to restore their faith in the establishment for, after a gruelling means test, they were offered a mite on condition that they repaid the British Government which, according to Milligan, might collapse with the loss of such a sum. On the whole he thought the Communist Party offer was more worthwhile.

However, they now had the fare to visit the Rocca family, rich friends of Toni Pontani, at their millionaire villa on Lake Maggiore. They spent some drunken days, and Spike fell in love with the daughter, Jean, while telling himself that he must make a determined bid for the favours of Lily Gibbs. They had completed their most successful tour (artistically) and returned to England with no soles on their shoes.

Eighteen Sorcerer's Apprentice?

*And will it be my fault
if things are so?*

Machiavelli

Milligan soon learned that most radio happened round a man called Jimmy Grafton, sometime scriptwriter for the BBC and host of the Grafton Arms, Victoria. People who mattered congregated there: performers, writers and producers. Grafton was a scriptwriter for the comedian, Derek Roy, who established *Variety Bandbox* as a huge favourite with the radio listeners of the late forties. It was when Michael Bentine joined the show that Grafton came to know him. Michael went on to the London Palladium, and later appeared in the radio show *Listen my Children* with Benny Hill and an unknown Peter Sellers.

It was Secombe who suggested to Spike that a visit to the Grafton Arms might be time well spent. Milligan wasn't too sure: he wanted to observe before getting involved; Spike is not afraid, he's cautious. He persuaded Grafton to let him help out behind the bar. In return, Grafton let him have an attic room and a bed where he covered himself with old coats and complained:

The world doesn't care if I live or die. . . .

Milligan was in his element. He was indulging that other side of the Irish, 'Pity, pity, for Christ's sake pity, before I take out a gun and shoot the whole bloody lot of yis!' Like many others of his race he believed that life was made up of plots. Two condemned men were discussing human values and one said that the only hope in a well-spent life was to accept anything a person could offer, even if that person had nothing more to give than his bootlaces. Milligan can't, or won't, think like that. With him it's all or nothing. To be a friend is to offer yourself as hostage to his moods. Having said which, of course, he will willingly die for you in return. Few people, however, have much use for personal martyrs.

I often wish, for Spike's sake, that all was altruism. Jimmy Grafton helped, but:

> He was using me as well. I was obviously writing superior comedy to him. I was acting as a barman. I used to make up these jokes and he'd say, 'I've never heard that joke,' and I'd say, 'Well, I make them up.' After a while he asked if I'd like to write with him, and I did. Yes, he was helping me, but he was also helping himself. But then I must say that he was a very generous man.

Maybe all people are reserved in their praise – most folk in show business certainly qualify their compliments to some extent. Like Secombe, for example, telling Sellers, who 'likes the name Milligan', that he will like the man as much as the name:

> He's one of us. A first-generation comic. He doesn't give a pig's eye about all that grease-paint aristocracy. The only trouble is, I should warn you, he is quite mad.[1]

I was interested in Michael Bentine's 'U' accent and demeanour but, according to Milligan, Bentine's 'old school tie' pose was 'nothing more than an act':

> He was only one year at Eton, but he displays the tie and the accent all the time now. Pretends to be Peruvian but he was born in Watford! A strange, weird man. He was full of ideas that became boring very quickly. Student humour.

One time Milligan had the idea that he'd do a book about the Goons to be called *Quartet*; and Bentine said that nobody could have his 'stuff' because everything he had done or said was classified. 'You see,' he told Spike, 'I was in MI5.'

> MI Five? He would have been lucky to have been let into MI One. He talks about fighting people in hand-to-hand combat and says, 'You know what it's like, Spike, when you've killed your first German.' But I don't remember what it was like killing my first German. I only remember being shit-scared in case I was killed by the first German that saw me.

It was around the early fifties that the genre of 'British Railways' jokes gained currency, and the National Health Service became the butt of every second-rate comic in Britain. The papers had declared war on the Welfare State and it became popular with audiences to criticize anything that wasn't owned and run for private profit. Spike says that Jimmy Grafton and the rest of the BBC Light Programme scriptwriters would try to drag a laugh from anything:

> *Jimmy was writing for a piss poor comic called Derek Roy who was as funny as a baby with cancer. I thought that original material that wasn't begging the laughs would be so much better, so I wrote a string of jokes for Grafton which he used in various radio programmes. Then, bit by bit, I wrote odd scripts of my own for radio and it was always around ten or twelve quid. I wrote for Alfred Marks, Harry Secombe, Bill Kerr, Dick Emery . . . for anybody needing a line. . . . Then The Goon Show started to emerge. I earned twelve pounds fifty for writing it, and the same for appearing in it . . . with the repeats I was on to about fifty pounds a week, which was big money in those days. Bloody marvellous money in 1953 – I suppose it would be like five hundred pounds a week nowadays. From then on I've never been poor, but I've never been able to stop.*

Milligan was making a very valid point. The wind of change that had swept through the staid corridors of the Third Programme and the Light had, more or less, passed radio comedy by – until *The Goon Show*. From the extra-mural studios of Sheriff's wine bar and the George public house, Dylan Thomas, Louis MacNeice and company had declared war on the moralistic White Anglo-Saxon Protestant image of the BBC.

A new force had come into broadcasting in the shape of Head of Features (Radio), Laurence Gilliam. A protégé of the great documentary film-maker John Grierson, Gilliam knew above all who to hire to write what. He commissioned MacNeice's *The Dark Tower* and *They Came on Good Friday*. He brought together Robert Graves, James Burns Singer and W. H. Auden, and he comforted and cajoled Dylan Thomas into writing *Under Milkwood*.

But away in the reaches of Aeolian Hall comedy didn't really want to change. Working-class people were funny because they slept in flat caps and kept coal in the bath. As for Milligan, had anybody really understood him in the beginning, he would never have got by the commissionaire.

Even at the height of *The Goon Show* Spike was in the wrong place at the right time. When Rene Peltier was head of the Light

Programme Spike wanted *The Goon Show* to be broadcast by them because it had a larger audience. The head of the Light wouldn't take the show and, at the time, Spike couldn't understand Peltier's decision. Years after *The Goon Show* had finished, Milligan and his long Irish memory were having a drink with Peltier. The now erstwhile head of the Light Programme told Spike that he and his wife hadn't really 'understood' *The Goon Show*. Milligan thinks that what Peltier meant to say was that he and his wife didn't 'like' *The Goon Show*, and for that reason it didn't go on:

> *It's like the Kremlin, the BBC – don't have any illusions about that.*

Maybe Spike was feeling a bit precious. Maybe he felt he was being singled out for special treatment. Not everybody in the BBC did his own thing. The poet MacNeice was a staff producer, but the poetry of Dylan Thomas was directed by Douglas Cleverdon. John Betjeman asked Gilliam 'if I might be allowed to twiddle the knobs for my bit myself?'

Everybody who was anybody, from Christopher Fry to Thomas Stearns Eliot, was made a little more famous by Laurence Gilliam and his people from Portland Place. And yet, despite the ease with which one rubbed shoulders with great men, Spike held poets like MacNeice and Robert Graves in awe, and still does. Wistfully, he sighs:

> *Wasn't MacNeice a fine poet? I was very mentally ill when I heard one of his last radio plays and I immediately phoned him up and said, 'I just wanted to tell you how much I enjoyed it.' At a loss he said, 'What?' And I said, 'I just wanted you to know how much I enjoyed your play.' And he said, 'Good' and hung up.*

When two writers, equally shy and introspective, try to speak ordinary words, the silence is bound to be deafening.

In the fifties, Harry Secombe brought what Milligan called in *Where Have All the Bullets Gone?* 'his insane jokes and raspberries' to the Nuffield Centre in London, and was very well received. So at Harry's instigation, Spike appeared there doing a solo act while still living at the Grafton Arms. The audience was mostly composed of members of the armed forces and Spike resolved to sing, play the guitar and tell stories about the war. He had gone there prepared to do a short spot, but his act went down so well that he was forced to prolong his appearance. He was amazed at the response:

> There was me, and my guitar, without even the trio or a script to hide behind, and I had an audience rolling in the aisles. Best of all I knew I was being funny because I could 'feel' the bits that the audience was laughing at.

Milligan, ever shrewd, learns his lessons well. A lesser comic would have taken a chance and depended again on his ability to do an unrehearsed show. Not Spike. Suddenly he understood the 'meaning' of collective humour. In future, for this man who takes his art so seriously, he would go on a stage and do an off-the-cuff performance based on very carefully prepared ad libs.

Harry Secombe was going from strength to strength, as was Michael Bentine. Sellers? that he should need a four-leaf clover? In the 1950s, the bigger the sound the better the occasion and each band had its speciality act. Milligan was touring American forces bases throughout England, appearing as the comic with Frank Weir and his Orchestra.

Back in Reigate, Desmond was in the middle of a three-year art course with Goldsmith's College. Flo was hankering after a warmer climate and Leo wasn't all that gone on democracy. He missed the perks of India where he was more equal than most. Spike told me that Leo and Flo used to drink nothing but shandies in Rangoon because they had been spoiled by champagne in Poona:

> The morning bread would arrive, and there'd be these bottles of champagne. Brought by the local bunnia [shopkeeper]. It was part of the perks that Dad got in exchange for letting him have the contract for supplying the regiment with gunny sacks, and the bunnia would bribe him with bottles of champagne. That's how it was done. My God! but my old man was fiddling the Indians all right.

Leo had never lost his passion for the stage and, now that Spike was beginning to be known, his father realized what he had missed. Spike seldom stayed at Leathwell Road now and this break made life almost unbearable for Leo. He collected every review, every scrap, and cherished every remark made about his son. It was a shame that Flo had stopped him going back on the stage. Spike tells of how he had brought back his dancing mat and his make-up box from India. Flo was terrified of the vagaries of a shameful profession – a man must have a decent job. Really, as her son believes, she worried that such a good-looking man might meet other women:

She was jealous of what might happen. And also she was matriarchal about being on the stage. She wouldn't want to tell the neighbours that her husband was a theatrical. A lot of snobbery in that, you know, because it wasn't regarded as a proper job. If Dad had just finished a successful week at the London Palladium, I think she would rather have told the neighbours that he was just back from working down the mines.

Then Leo learned that the fare to the Antipodes was nearly as cheap as it had been during the days of transportation. So it was agreed that Flo and Leo and Desmond and Kathleen would emigrate to Australia, just as soon as the youngest son graduated from art school. Desmond put his head down and vowed to emerge from Goldsmith's College a star pupil.

Attlee went to the country in 1950 on the old Tory-favouring register and his majority was reduced from 146 to 6. In an effort to placate the Tory press his new Chancellor of the Exchequer, Hugh Gaitskell, imposed a charge of one shilling on prescriptions. The Minister of Health, Aneurin Bevan, described Gaitskell as 'a desiccated calculating machine' and resigned from office. He was joined on the left wing of the Labour Party by his old comrade, the Oxford militant socialist, firebrand Harold Wilson.

Attlee went to the country again in 1951, and while Labour polled nearly a quarter of a million more votes than the opposition, the Conservatives came back to power with a majority of 26.

Meanwhile, Spike tells how Leo saw his first Pakistani bus conductor in Lewisham and, with the slogan 'I don't want to get bleeding small-pox', he went home and ordered the family to pack for Australia. Was Spike joking?

Joking? No I'm not joking. Dad was a fascist. Even in Australia it caught up with him. I was sitting with him one day watching television and on comes an aborigine corroboree – of course in Australia the aborigines are kept for the most part in

> *the outback. So Dad looks up and says, 'Where's all these niggers from, Spike?' 'They're not niggers,' I told him. 'Yes they are, they're fucking black the same as niggers.' 'They're Australian,' I told him, 'aboriginals.' 'I don't care what they call them, son, they'll be sorry they ever let the bastards in because they breed like rabbits.'*

Much as Milligan hated the Conservative Party he was shrewd enough to realize that *The Goon Show* would have had no real focus without them in power. Indeed goonery lasted only as long as the Tory administration, which endured, it is incredible to recall, for thirteen years without a break.

His brother and parents had hardly reached Australia when Joe Loss, the bandleader, asked Spike to tour with him. It was a godsend. Milligan had been in the throes of despair when the approach was made. He had been contacted by the BBC to do a pilot for a new series with his new humour, to be written round him and his friends. Nobody at the staid Beeb knew how to react to this totally surrealist form of comedy, and what the establishment doesn't understand it destroys.

Joe Loss, always one of the fairest of men in show business, did what only a very great man will do; he allowed Spike to have his own well-promoted spot with all the support of the band. Spike took every advantage of the occasion and soon his reputation was spreading throughout the country. Despite the mass appeal of radio, this was still the big band era when dancing was the thing.

Milligan was nowadays living in a room in Peg Sellers' house, and it was just as well since he felt that his family had deserted him. Even today, he feels that it was her support which kept him going through the frustrating periods of waiting for the BBC bureaucracy to make up its established mind.

Then, Jimmy Grafton, Pat Dixon, and that wonderful man of radio and TV entertainment, Denis Main Wilson, got together with Milligan and company to make a new pilot which was to be called *Those Crazy People*. The pilot was accepted and the show went out on 28th May, 1951.

Nineteen The Goon Show

*Goons and ginks and company
Finks.*

Joe Hill, *Union Maid*

Even before *Crazy People* was renamed *The Goon Show* in June
1952, it was obvious that Spike Milligan had outgrown the sound
of art. It was as if he had tapped the 'ineluctable modality of the
audible' and he was concerned with something else. From May
1951 until *The Last Smoking Seagoon* was broadcast in January
1960, the show was a millstone but, even by the time the first
programme in the second series was due to be transmitted, he
had lost all but manic interest in the proceedings.

Like a child with a new toy, the moment Milligan discovers
how it works, he wants to put it aside and play with something
else. Besides which, his girl-friend of some four years, June Marlowe, asked if he would agree to marry her before she left for
Australia with her parents. They were wed on 26th January,
1952 and Milligan was so haunted by the Goons that he hardly
noticed her departure for the Antipodes.

Spike himself was staggered by the public reaction to his audi-
tory surrealism. Throughout the country the most unlikely folk
were going around imitating the crazy people. In school Prince
Charles was driving his fellows mad with his impersonations of
'Bluebottle'. Everybody thought they knew what 'Minnie',
'Crun', and 'Bloodnok' looked like and no two images were the
same. This is as it should be since the Goons were disembodied
voices – more and nothing more than that. Wireless, a new and
underdeveloped medium even today, had for years been in the
power of people who, but for the decline in, and eventual loss
of, the Empire, would have been pursuing useless careers in
the Colonial Service. And then suddenly one thing begat another. There was no single catalyst unless we can blame it on the
war.

The British Broadcasting Company had been set up in 1922

with John Reith as its general manager. It broadcast a concert on record from a Hampstead garden in July of that same year, treating its listeners to what was described as 'an entertainment of unconsidered trifles of the lightest type'. Not very British, but typically English understatement.

By 1927 the British Broadcasting Corporation, a publicly financed company and ultimately responsible to parliament, was given a monopoly covering all phases of broadcasting in Britain. Sir John Reith became its first director general. It was an interesting appointment and it seemed that if broadcasting was to be the mouthpiece of the new religion in the UK then it was preferable to find a Holy Ghost of the true and established faith. Such a religious being could only be found in Scotland, where all that is joyful is sinful. In John Reith the establishment chose well: a rough, tough Glaswegian whose first instinct was to beat up his enemies. When Reith learned that his father had been knocked down in the street, Roger Milner says he felt a useless, unproductive anger which caused him to rush 'round Glasgow clutching a heavy spanner, determined to brain the van driver who'd run over his father'.[1]

The stories about Reith's middle-class minister morals are legion. They range from an announcer who was dismissed because he read the news in a lounge suit instead of evening dress, to a man who was not permitted to read the 'Epilogue' because he was divorced. And yet, Reith brooked no interference from any quarter, and during his stewardship he built into the Corporation an independence which was jealously guarded until the advent of Yuppie politics and the second coming of Thatcher.

If the BBC paid scant attention to party politics, Spike Milligan saw the doings of parliament as fair game. He told Pauline Scudamore that he had never been influenced by Kafka or Ionescu, or even Dylan Thomas: 'I got my influences listening to Members of Parliament making fools of themselves in the House of Commons. . . . '[2]

It was popularly believed that, within the Corporation, nobody above the level of producer ever listened to the Light Programme or the Home Service. Whatever truth there is in that notion, it really is incredible that anything as artistic as *The Goon Show* should have lasted as long as it did. It was all right for the BBC Third – that was filled with nuts like Dylan Thomas, Louis MacNeice, David Thompson, and trendy left-wing poets to whom nobody except other lunatics ever listened – until *Under Milkwood,* that is.

Spike talks of 'straight' comedy and then compares that with how he saw *The Goon Show:*

> *Goonery is quite a different thing altogether. The establishment isn't into goonery. Therefore, the people who owned and ran the BBC appreciated the listening figures they were getting – which was good for them to keep their jobs. But they still don't know about goonery. They never knew we were sending up bureaucracy – they still don't.*

Arthur Askey got work because he was a midget Liverpudlian with a quaint accent that was made even more odd by Richard Murdoch's standard public school tones:

> *They're a lot of square-cuts at the Beeb – some are even hexamerous. Arthur Haines was a step in the right direction – a sort of less sophisticated Tony Hancock. All thanks to Johnny Speight who first started the idea of the down-trodden man, the socially deprived person: the tramp.*

But people like Johnny, Spike thinks, are mistaken if they believe that the BBC or any of the other companies care over-much about standards:

> *Politics are not purveyed as such in comedy. You asked did I do the Irish Pakistani bus conductor because I wanted to send up the English stories about the Irish. Nothing so noble. I just thought it was an incredible mixture. I try out new characters, new techniques, partly because I get bored very quickly. A comic is always the first person to laugh at his own joke and it's difficult to enjoy something when you've heard it before.*

What was wrong with broadcasting companies? Why is there apparently perpetual conflict between them and their artistes?

> *Broadcasting is limited by being human and they don't have a department of imagination at the Beeb at all. I mean, if it was left to the BBC Van Gogh would never have painted anything but scenery.*

The powers that be had enough on their plates trying to explain a Welsh village, the name of which looked innocent enough until you looked at it backwards. Oh Dylan, you beauty! What a shock for the gnomes on the sixth floor of Broadcasting House! None of them even knew there was life after Luxembourg on the dial. And now here was this horrible drunken poet talking about buggerall but sex as though everybody suffered from it. Thank God he was but a cunning Celt! Oh, had he been Godforbid English, and not an expendable Welshman! Then there would have been the flak from the radio listeners' watch committee and all those of promiscuous morality who creep in such petty places.

For a while the memos fell from the Beeb Boardroom like ticker-tape on a Broadway circus. Who, they demanded, had dared rock the boat? The Third had been created to keep a minority audience quiet, and now millions were eavesdropping in the hope of hearing the word arse pronounced art, or vice versa, and oh, that horrible vice versa. Where it would all end only God and Kenneth Tynan knew.

Milligan's salvation was that the brass understood him less than they understood the recondite radio of the Third programme. And indeed who could blame them when Milligan himself described his dramatis personae thus:

> Major Denis Bloodnok (*Military Idiot, Coward and Bar*) . . . *found wearing false testicles* . . .: *Willium 'Mate' Cobblers*. *'Now uniformed doorman at Aeolian Hall wears full war medals at all times'*: *Hercules Grytype-Thynne, the Hon*. *'(A plausible public school villain and cad)'*: *Comte Toulouse-Moriarty of the House of Roland '*. . . *bald daft deaf and worthless.'*[3]

Eccles is 'the original goon', Neddy Seagoon 'a true British idiot and hero always'. Bluebottle is 'a cardboard cut-out liquorice and string hero', while Minnie Bannister is 'Spinster of this Parish'. Mr Henry Crun doesn't know who he is.

> CRUN: (*hysteria*) Stop it – ahhh – stop that crazy rhythm, you sinful woman. (*vapours*) Aahhhh – oooooh – now lets get on with the work. Have you cleared that E flat pipe yet?
> MINNIE: Yes buddy – try it.
> GRAMS: ONE OR TWO TOOTS ON ORGAN.
> SPIKE: Hear that sound listeners – huh?[4]

Milligan never for a second forgot that the listener was just there at the end of the microphone. Together they made the play, and the success of *The Goon Show* owed a great deal to the idea of taking the audience into his confidence.

But, by 1952, a prisoner of the Goons, Milligan was in the throes of despair: writing the scripts and appearing in the series was taking every minute of his waking and sleeping life. He had been living rough before his bride, June, went (pregnant) to Australia: then, with her time near, she wanted to come home. June was a beautiful woman, but quite impractical. Spike didn't have a home, and he was so badly paid by the BBC that there didn't seem to be any immediate prospect of him being able to afford one. And so, until they could buy a place of their own, Milligan rented a flat from real estate relations of Sellers.

On the 2nd November, 1952, Laura Milligan was born and, shortly afterwards, her father realized that June was really a sexy version of David Copperfield's Dora. Property prices in the fifties were such that for one thousand pounds a couple could have bought a decent house, a deposit of as little as one hundred pounds could have secured a home. Painfully Spike scraped together five hundred pounds and relaxed somewhat – even if the bottom fell out of the broadcasting business he and his wife had at least security of tenure. The rest of the story is even worse than the one he tells about Rosy and her scrap-dealing husband:

> '*That money I gave yeh, June, to keep safe for our future home, can I have it now?*'
>
> '*Oh, Jazes, Spike, I gave it to a nice man who told me that I'd have ballroom dancing lessons for the rest of my life.*'

Milligan told me that, for a moment, he believed he was rehearsing an incident in the crazy life of the Goons. It was inevitably his 'own fault':

> *June had been used to money and was an easy mark for a glib salesman.*

But five hundred pounds should have been a drop in the ocean to the man who was, according to his friend, Eric Sykes, doing the work of three men each week. As time went on Spike almost dispensed with the help he had been receiving from Eric Sykes and Larry Stephens: he had become one of the most accomplished writers for radio in the country.

For a man with his responsibilities and meagre rewards he coped well. Oh, due to overwork and family stress he had the occasional nervous breakdown to stop him going round the bend. Indeed, during 1953-4 he went frequently back and forth to the psychiatric wing of St Luke's Hospital. The number of poems he wrote while attending St Luke's bears witness to support his contention that many of his best poems were composed while undergoing psychiatric care. During a nervous breakdown in Bournemouth in 1967 he wrote a poem in which I think he gets nearer a description of the turmoil in his head than in any other work:

> The flowers in my garden
>   grow down.
> Their colour is pain
> Their fragrance sorrow.
> Into my eyes grow their roots
>   feeling for tears
> To nourish the black
>   Hopeless rose
>   Within me.[5]

But even in that he was fortunate since he had friends like Sykes who would stand in at the drop of a mental depression. Eric is the only show business personality I have ever heard Milligan refer to without reservation: Sykes has been an admiring friend from whom Spike learned a great deal, and who, nonetheless, appreciated the genius of Milligan. They are political opposites, but the bond of comradeship between Eric Sykes and Spike Milligan has never even been strained.

Not that Milligan does not appreciate his other friendships. Harry Secombe recognized the burden that was on Spike's shoulders during the Goon years. He has said on more than one occasion that while he and Sellers and Bentine could walk away after the recording, Milligan was still left behind to get the whole show on the road for the following week. Sellers knew also the outrageous hours his friend was putting in each week to make the programme work. Milligan may never have told them so in so many words, but he was deeply touched by the loyalty of Sellers and Secombe; Harry might have some grand ideas, but he was a totally lovable and generous man. Their foibles fascinated Milligan:

Peter was a bit woolly in the head. One day he could be a Jew, next day a spiritualist: by the end of the week he became a Methodist. He vacillated vastly in his life. He never quite knew what he was. It was the result of being brought up by a Jewish mother who had lost her religion, and a Protestant father who was so slightly troubled by Christianity that he sent Peter to a Catholic school.

Peter Sellers' spiritualism convinced him that Dan Leno was guiding his career from the grave. He had what Milligan calls a 'totally non-scholastic education'. 'Show business was all he ever knew.' He didn't know if either he or Secombe had ever read a book because he hadn't seen any in their houses and, since Bentine had never invited him to his home, he couldn't be too sure about his reading habits.

Sellers was fascinated by clothes. Spike says he was 'mad to look good'. He wore 'every accoutrement from the tailor except the ticket of sale . . . You never saw such a bloody mess':

He wore gloves, a trilby hat – if there'd been a face-mask he'd have worn one of those as well. He'd leave his raincoat open to show that he had a single-breasted jacket underneath – thereby getting his inner self wet at the same time. He was very nice and very strange. Quite mad. He and Secombe were mad. They said I was mad but I was the only one with a reason.

And yet, despite Peter's penchant for the sartorial, he used to buy shoes without laces so that he would not have to bend down 'to tie them up'. Milligan says that he was so lazy he paid for it in the end:

He was in training for a heart attack from the age of twenty onwards. He ate everything that was fat and his mother told him always to rest and never overwork himself. He never did any exercise and I think he'd be alive today if he had. Isn't that a real Irish one – 'He'd be alive today if it wasn't for the fact that he's dead'?

Sellers, he says, was innocent in many ways. He was a very great actor, a very funny actor; but did I know that Spike had given him scripts which he had screwed up?

That's right, great and all as he was he had to be told what a script was about, didn't know what was funny and what wasn't

. . . one of those things . . . He could read words, but not meanings.

He was very funny, though.

. . . Used to ring me up and make me laugh a lot about his descriptions of people, beautifully observed. Very Swiftian . . . and he hated Americans with such a venom, you'd have thought he was Red Indian on his parents' side.

Milligan and June had two more children, Sean born in 1954 and Sile two years his junior. He says that he wasn't paying enough attention to June, and it came as a shock but no great surprise when in the summer of 1959, while visiting his parents and divorced brother, Desmond, in Australia, he received word from a friend that she was sueing him for divorce.

He tried to persuade his wife to stay but she said that she had met somebody else. Spike eventually got custody of the children and comforted himself with the thought that through his own neglect he had lost his wife. Were he and June too young? Did he live as Shaw said a writer must – by neglecting his family in the interests of literature? Nobody but Terence Alan and June Milligan can answer that: suffice to say that while he was pacifying bank managers he counted forty pairs of shoes belonging to June; but what's the point of dancing lessons if you don't have the footwear for them?

Shortly before his divorce, Milligan had become a member of that amorphous body known as the Campaign for Nuclear Disarmament. He had met with Michael Foot on an Aldermaston march and been introduced to Bertrand Russell. Having suffered numerous breakdowns because of the pressure of broadcasting, he suddenly realized through the CND that the world had more to worry it.

Maybe the realization of the size of the nuclear threat began to put things in perspective, maybe not; but had it not been for his involvement with the anti-bomb movement of the period, it is probably correct to assume that his parting from June would have been much more traumatic than it actually was. Certainly he had come to terms with his personal problems much better than previously. When, for example, he had asked the hypnotherapist, Joe Robson, for help in 1955.

Robson had only agreed to see Milligan after Mrs Robson had

pleaded Spike's case. He was not a fan of *The Goon Show*, he didn't like the humour because it seemed to be beyond his comprehension. When he did finally meet with Milligan it didn't please him to learn that Spike didn't have much faith in doctors. It pleased him even less to hear Spike's anti-Semitic jokes. He told Milligan:

> *If I am to treat you, it will be a question of fifty-fifty, half your effort and half mine.*[6]

Robson persuaded Spike to relax and think about something pleasant that would help him reach a degree of tranquillity. Milligan fell asleep speaking of India. Afterwards, of course, the hypnotherapist, hypnotized by Milligan's charms, knew that:

> *He's not at all anti-Semitic, but he will make these terrible racist and anti-Semitic jokes. And then I do get cross. After all, I am a Jew. And, he demeans himself in a way, doesn't he?*[7]

Milligan, already under extreme pressure from the BBC who were paying him less per week than the wages of a production assistant, now heard that his producer, Peter Eton, was threatening to join Independent Television. He had been the first director with whom Spike was on the same wavelength:

> *Most producers had all the charisma of an out-of-order phone box. They sat there and pressed knobs and buttons, but doing no more than might be normally expected from any reasonably intelligent person. The one that was different was Peter Eton. He was the one guy that used to beat the shit out of the sound-effects boys to get the right atmosphere. Before Peter all we ever had was door-knocks, bell-rings, and feet on gravel. . . .*

The threatened departure of Eton affected him, it seems, much more than the news from June that she wanted a divorce.

Twenty The Swinging Sixties

> *O wad some power the giftie gie us*
> *To see oursels as others sees us . . .*

Robert Burns

My mother is Minnie, and Crun was really Leo, but not on the same level as my father. Crun was the invention of a solicitor we knew, and the company he was with was called Wacklo, Fuddle and Crun. Crun was always full of deeds, documents and the dead. The conversation between Henry and Minnie was really based on my father and mother who used to talk to each other and not listen – from separate rooms: they never listened to each other.

No, he hadn't known how popular *The Goon Show* had been:

Nobody had ever thought to tell me. But then they were all egocentrics like Sellers. Secombe especially wanted to be on his own; didn't want to think that he owed the Goons anything. Harry wanted to make it without bowing the knee to anybody, but I think the show gave him a big lift in his career.

Just two months after *The Goon Show* finished in 1960, Spike was awarded custody of his children and he heaved a sigh of relief. He now had to settle down and earn a new living for himself and three kids. For a while he wouldn't be able to afford the luxury of going mad.

The Goon Show had taught Milligan many lessons, the most important being that professional writers cannot afford to wait on the Muse. Be like Marghanita Laski and take inspiration from your typewriter, for trying to kick the mercurial daughters of Zeus up the arts is a thankless task. Bentine, for example, brought what he had learned to his Square World, having left *The Goon Show* after the second series. People have suggested that Michael and the other goons quarrelled but Spike swears that is not so.

He wasn't the most sociable person in the world and he never mixed like the rest of us, but he was a very funny man.

Everything went into the Goons, for Spike uses every experience. All for the good of the show and nothing was sacred. Actors became indistinguishable from the characters he created for them. He exploited their personal mannerisms and foibles – Bentine's self-indulgence, Secombe's manic exuberance, Sellers' painful need to meet life in the persona of anybody else rather than himself:

> *Sleeping or waking, I used any consciousness. Dreams are of particular interest because, in them, life is so disembodied. Let me explain what I mean. This very strange dream I had quite recently: I dreamt I was on duty at Oxford Circus. I was dressed like a traffic warden, and I had a stick with a mirror on the end of it, and I was holding it under women's skirts and saying to them that I was a 'knicker warden'. It seemed to be reasonable and proper as it does in all dreams. I was acting in accordance with some law that said if women weren't wearing knickers they weren't allowed to cross the street. Now I can't believe that dream – but I had it.*

A psychoanalyst would suggest that there is no discrepancy between Spike's dream-images and what passes for external reality in *The Goon Show*. In *The Mighty Wurlitzer*, for example, Milligan's obsession with legs is given such rein that the whole episode is almost hallucinated fantasy:

GRYTPYPE-THYNNE: Not so fast, crazy-type frog-eater. Neddie? Allow me to introduce my heavily oiled friend, Count Fred Moriarty, crack leather bucaine player and voted Mr Thin Legs of 1912.

MORIARTY: Correction, Thin Leg.

GRYTPYPE-THYNNE: Leg?

MORIARTY: Yes, I only entered one. Now, Seagoon – tell us, what is that fifty-ton brass-bound contraption you're driving?

SEAGOON: It's a Wurlitzer.

MORIARTY: We thought it was a mirage.

SEAGOON: A mirage? I've never heard of that make. Ha ha. (!)[1]

In 1924, André Breton defined surrealism:

> *Pure psychic automatism which is intended to express, verbally,*
> *in writing or by other means, the real process of thought.*
> *Thought's dictation, in the absence of all control exercised*
> *by the reason and outside all aesthetic and moral*
> *preoccupations.*[2]

Thought through the eyes?

Accepting that Milligan in describing his dreams does not deliberately edit or improve on them so as to make them more plausible or coherent, it is reasonable to accept that Spike's waking creative moments are almost as uninhibited as are his unconscious ones. Few writers are able to free themselves from their inhibitions in this way, and it is interesting to note that, like Milligan, many of the surrealists, Breton, René Crevel, Philip Soupault, for example, slept badly. So did some of the 'stream of consciousness' writers, like James Joyce, Louis Aragon and Virginia Woolf.

How much of Milligan is bound up in the unconscious, be he awake or asleep? How much of what he 'dreams' is intentional? He seems ambivalent about the way he uses dreams in his work:

> *I'm always baffled by them. It's all very strange . . . I don't*
> *think we know enough about ourselves. We might be learning*
> *more about the universe but, as to the actual mind . . . the way*
> *the mind thinks . . .*

Sinister dreams seemed to hang about like after-shock:

> *I dreamt I was condemned to death for something, and before*
> *my execution they said, 'Oh, you have to eat this chocolate*
> *elephant.' And I was there eating this huge chocolate elephant*
> *which was in the well of the court – it was so big that I had to*
> *get up a ladder to eat it. Then, it was gone, ladder, elephant,*
> *court-room and all . . . very strange . . .*

Epiphany for a *Goon Show* script? Or was the elephant India and the disappointment at England not being the land of chocolate and ice cream?

Milligan, a natural poet, maintains that much of his poetry is written in the realm of the unconscious; that is, he says that he writes some poetry while he is in a state of manic depression. But how did he become a poet in the first place?

Most writers learn by trial and error: by, during a lifetime,

151

writing all the rubbish out of themselves. Spike had served his time as a rhymster and, partly through making uncountable, unspeakable limericks, he had learned all about writing verse – or rather he had learned all that he should have learned about writing verse. Or maybe he had learned how not to write verse. His mind, uncluttered by pedagogic confusion, was still nearly brand new when it tackled *Silly Verses for Kids,* with the faces of his absent children standing in for the muses, since many of the poems had been written before Laura, Sean and Sile were restored to him by the courts. One of the latest poems he published in *The Mirror Running* illustrates the hard grasp his art has on his mind:

'The Sea'

Monstrous, mechanical, timeless,
* calm to cruel infinity,*
Sightless, black, borne deep,
Sucked-down sailors
* filled with sunken dreams.*
Black the women stand
* on grief-clutched shores.*
Fishermen, fishermen,
* where are your songs?*
Silent in water-stopped mouths,
Fathomed skulls
* unthink their yesterdays.*
Did divine feet once walk on you,
* or were you just being kind?*

(Pevensey, May 1986)[3]

Echoes of 'Riders to the Sea'? – and yet Spike had never read his fellow countryman. But he, too, like Synge, was a playwright. It was good, therefore, that he formed a lasting friendship with Bernard Miles and his Thameside Mermaid Theatre. Miles was that unique actor-manager who could see and admire creative genius without confusing the role of the performing arts. He knew the stories about Milligan; that Spike was difficult to work with, that he tended to rewrite scripts and give fellow actors a hard time with ad libs, etc. He found Spike to be a disciplined and dedicated actor of real genius and swore that the part of Ben

152

Gunn in the Mermaid adaptation of *Treasure Island* had been made for Spike.

During the winter of 1961–2, and while *Treasure Island* was running, Spike and Bernard Miles talked about a play to be set in a post-nuclear world. It would be called *The Bed-Sittingroom* and it was to be written by Spike in collaboration with John Antrobus who, said Miles (in the best West-country dialect), should know about such things as destruction because he:

> *Woz at Sandherst and that iz wear he lernt a lot of stuf that iz in thiz play.*[4]

Some time later, Lord Miles (as he became) was talking to me in his office at the Mermaid and, looking up at a photograph of Milligan in Ben Gunn costume, he said admiringly:

> *Few actors ever put so much into a part and got so much more out.*[5]

In *The Bed-Sittingroom* Milligan showed that the best dialogue written is made to be spoken when Captain Pontius Kak shouts through a loud-hailer at Lord Fortnum of Alamein:

> *Lord Fortnum, as your doctor, I must advise strongly against the taking of prayer!*[6]

The work of the nineteenth-century Russian writer, Ivan Aleksandrovich Goncharov, was soon high on Milligan's hit list. Nor would he be the first to find gold in that vein; before Milligan there had been other prospectors like Ionesco and Beckett, but only Spike, it would seem, got into Goncharov's mind and into that of his great character Oblomov.

Goncharov satirized the Russian court and, in particular, St Petersburg society, and Oblomov embodied all the characteristic traits of laziness and ineffectiveness which hastened the decline of the Holy Russian empire.

When Spike's version first opened at the Lyric Hammersmith, London, on 6th October, 1964, it didn't work. All there on the page it lacked breath and blood. The actors were unhappy and the audience was nervous. For the first two performances it looked as if the producer, Frank Dunlop, had a disaster on his hands. On the third night, Milligan began to interpret Goncharov as the mood took him, thereby, through genius or sheer serendipity, playing the part as the novelist would probably have intended. After a record-breaking run (for the Lyric) of six weeks, the show transferred to the Comedy Theatre in the West End in triumph, as *Son of Oblomov*, which indeed it was.

And yet, changing the course of Oblomov had not been easy; it had not been a question of 'with one bound gallant Jack was free'; some of the actors with whom Spike worked during the hilarious run of Oblomov objected to his interpolations. They complained that he was still making the dialogue up as he went along but, according to Milligan, the only reason he was changing the script was because some actors hadn't bothered to learn their lines in the first place.

Milligan is a song-writer, a journalist, an essayist. According to the criteria laid down by Carlyle he is an historian, since his memoirs are basically the biographies of great men, from Tony Goldsmith to Bill Hall to the Eighth Army. But, is he a novelist? Again, like Professor Joad, one is forced to say, 'It all depends on what you mean.'

According to the Oxford English Dictionary, the novel is:

> *A fictitious prose narrative or tale of considerable length . . . in which characters and actions representative of the real life of past or present times are portrayed in a plot of more or less complexity.*

Now there is a nice Jesuitical definition if I've ever read one. Some leery lexicographer, having arrived at a typically cloistered conclusion, suddenly remembers Homer and Joyce, Stendhal and Dostoevski, Tolstoy and Dickens. Fiction, like parralax, is all in the eye of the observer. So, while Milligan's 1987 novel, *The Loony*, is the history of an Irish Oblomov, his first narrative tale, *Puckoon* is a version of Irish history.

Milligan began to write *Puckoon* after he had met Patricia Ridgeway, to whom he was married on 28th April, 1962. First published in 1963, *Puckoon*, like *Silly Verses for Kids* some four years previously, was very well received. This was the period in British politics commonly comically called 'caring capitalism'. Macmillan told us we never had it so good while Milligan assured the world that there were some who never had it at all.

In Britain, we were living in the last openly class-conscious society. In the arts, too. Frank Norman was a 'working-class' writer just as the chap who wrote the music for his shows, Lionel Bart, was a 'working-class' composer. There was Alan Sillitoe and Harold Pinter and Shelagh Delaney. In the performing arts the people were represented by O'Toole and Finney, Finlay, Courtenay and Bell.

It wasn't a good time for Noël Coward's happy breed. Their stage had been stolen by Joan Littlewood's Theatre Workshop version of Brecht's *Berliner Ensemble*, and four lads from Liverpool were about to pull the piano stool from under Novello.

But, since every action has its reaction, there was the other side of the coin. Cambridge Footlights had hijacked the satire business just as their political fellows stole the Labour Party. From now on, through *Beyond the Fringe, Monty Python, That Was The Week That Was*, and Harold Wilson, it would be a question of the bland leading the bland. The only one to avoid class definition was Spike Milligan. His work was unique.

It was at this time that the establishment retook the BBC from the post-war avant-garde. The Milligans and the Thomases and the R. D. Smiths and the MacNeices had scared the living daylights out of them. To the shame of unthinking pamphleteers the bureaucracy retook its citadel and replaced 'politics without art' with their version of 'art without politics'. The sixth floor of Broadcasting House made it clear. From now on the barricades would be taken down, the barriers restored, and a proper discrimination achieved. It was to be us and them, Dud and Pete, Alf Garnett, and Hercules the Horse.

Milligan has always puzzled over why his brilliant 'Q' series, which began in the late sixties, never achieved the same television fame as the Goons did on radio. He doesn't know that when the establishment takes a genuine genre created by genius, the only way it can use it for its own amusement is in a debased form. Sub Milligan is acceptable, Spike Milligan is not. Wilde, bowdlerized by 'Coward Codology', is safer than having to live with Oscar's politics as well as his wit.

Harold Wilson, pledged to emulate John Kennedy's '100 days of dynamic action', dissolved Parliament in March 1966 and in the ensuing election Labour was returned with a majority of 94. Two months later, Spike's fourth child, Jane, was born on 17th May.

Spike visited his brother and parents in Australia in 1969, and had just returned to England when his father died following a stroke. He had had a good innings, but that didn't make it any easier on Spike.

Twenty-one Who Goes with Fergus?

And no more turn aside and brood
Upon love's bitter mystery
For Fergus rules the brasen cars.

W. B. Yeats

Milligan had nothing for which to reproach himself after his father's death. But that did little to ease his grief. Only just before he died did Leo reveal to Spike that his own life had been a private hell; he had, it appeared, because of despair, spent years in mental isolation, in a sort of self-imposed solitary confinement.

Spike had done his duty as a son and, when in a position to supply their needs, had never left his parents wanting. And then, too, his father and mother had been able, for a little while, to enjoy Spike's fame together.

Flo had almost come to terms with the stage. Acting and immorality were not any longer necessarily synonymous. On occasion she was even prepared to admit to her own early career in theatre. In a letter to Spike she says:

> *My! fancy! my eldest boy . . . West End! . . . never thought in*
> *the days when Dad and I . . . and our concert parties . . . that*
> *one day . . . our son Terence . . . his name in lights . . . but your*
> *credit is due to you and you alone and may God and His Blessed*
> *Mother look after you from success to success . . . Dad and I*
> *feel quite sure of that. . . .*

And she enclosed yet another miraculous medal.

Making a voyage round his father, Spike re-read Leo's correspondence and wondered about the memories of the past:

> *Maybe the letters of the dead should be sent to the dead letter*
> *office?*

The feelings of guilt. Could he have done more? Been more understanding? Milligan tortured himself in the wake of his father. Cheery, happy Leo had always been there whenever Spike needed help. Even from twelve thousand miles away he had watched over his Terry, consoled his every care. Only when he wanted to reassure his sick son did he reveal to Spike that, throughout his entire life, he too had been a manic depressive.

He had concealed it from Flo and the children because there was nothing anybody could do about it then.

> *There was no relief for my suffering, no drugs, or psychiatrists.*
> *. . . It was 'Cold Turkey' for me all the way . . .*
>
> *I left home at the age of fourteen and had very little contact*
> *with my father and mother after that . . . My school days were*
> *a torment, my army days were worse . . .*
>
> *Civilian life brought no relief . . . I worked a twelve-hour*
> *day . . . sixteen hours on Sunday, with disreputable men*
> *and women whom I loathed . . . I must have had some Irish*
> *O'Maolagain toughness in my moral fibre that carried me*
> *through . . .*
>
> *Can you wonder then, that all my life from early childhood,*
> *I envied the character, Robinson Crusoe, alone and away from*
> *the torment of a hard and cruel world? . . . Our combined love*
> *to you our son, God and His Blessed Mother keep you safe and*
> *well.*[1]

In another letter, written shortly before leaving Australia for a holiday with Spike and his family, God was on shaky ground. Leo confessed that he had lost faith, but not completely. There was still a spark left, which might be rekindled again before he passed on, but at that moment he wasn't sure.

Spike read and re-read Leo's 'calendars' and, almost without thinking, began to recall his own army days:

> *It had been like 'a Cook's Tour without ever costing me a*
> *penny'.*

He decided to research his war memoirs. He was now an accomplished artiste in the Chaplin mould – he was a performer, singer, musician, composer, writer and playwright:

> *Those bastards in BBC wouldn't let me direct. I'll never forget*
> *that sanctimonious, parsimonious, acrimonious Huw Wheldon.*
> *Wrote to tell me how much he enjoyed me – but wouldn't let me*
> *direct; oh no, I wasn't wearing the proper tie for that.*

Wheldon was Head of Documentary and Musical programmes and the show he was so enthusiastic about was *Muses with*

Milligan. It was the first television programme to mix poetry and jazz successfully. Much as Wheldon liked his style he had no intention of encouraging Spike to become a director:

> *I wrote to him and he said, 'No, no, we have plenty of our own people waiting to become directors.' His own people? How the hell did he expect us all to have been at the same school? There wouldn't have been enough room.*

He was a recording artiste: in the fifties, Milligan could be played on twenty-one discs from 78″ to LP; the sixties could hear him on nineteen records. Milligan today has nearly a hundred recordings to his credit.

Since his first radio appearance with the Bill Hall Trio in 1947, Milligan has starred in countless radio and television productions including *The Goons*, *The Telegoons* and the 'Q' series which ended with *Q9* in 1980.

He has appeared in twenty-seven films, published six volumes of verse, thirty volumes of prose and one play: *The Bed-Sittingroom* (with John Antrobus). He can hold the stage with his one-man show in as professional a manner as either of the two 'legitimate' stage artists he admired most, Michael MacLiammoir and Peter Ustinov. Poet, playwright and novelist, Milligan's talent stretches the meaning of versatility, and demands new superlatives.

I said to him that he was an artist's artist and he begged me not to make my opinion public:

> *They give me little enough work as it is . . .*

He is a teacher, reluctant maybe, but a teacher nevertheless. From him had the young men of *Beyond the Fringe* and *Monty Python* learned their trade. They made no bones about it, and never denied their debt to Milligan. In particular, Terry Jones, Michael Palin and Terry Gilliam. The writers of *Monty Python* said:

> *Watching Q5, we almost felt as if our guns had been Spiked! We had been writing quickies or sketches for some three years and they always had a beginning, a middle and a tag line. Suddenly, watching Spike Milligan, we realized that they didn't have to be like that.*[2]

Equally generous, John Cleese told David Nathan that 'Milligan is the great God of us all.'

Just as coming across Bertrand Russell had led him to give up meat, working with the selfless Robert Graves, persuaded Milligan to take his poetry seriously. And, realizing that the broadcasting organizations and the BBC in particular had ruthlessly exploited him, he thought: This is wrong and must not happen to everybody else. He looked around and, seeing fellow writers like Johnny Speight, John Antrobus, Ray Galton and Alan Simpson being ripped off, he got them to band together in Associated London Scripts for their protection.

It didn't work out because few people are as unselfish as Spike – Eric Sykes being a notable exception:

> *I could never repay Eric, not if I lived to be a thousand.*

His experience with some of his fellow writers in Associated London Scripts affected Milligan very badly. Some of those he had sought to help had come to deals behind Spike's back and with little regard for his well-being. And yet, despite that episode, it was in the sixties that Milligan really flowered.

It was as if he realized it had been a special era in history. Beginning with Harold Macmillan declaring: 'The class war is obsolete', the decade had ended with John Lennon asserting: 'The people who are in control and in power and the class system and the whole bullshit bourgeois scene is exactly the same.'

The same? Yes, but different. The Lord Chamberlain's Office had been done away with and the Obscene Publications Act thrashed in the High Court. Anybody who wanted to read *Lady Chatterley's Lover* could do so without fear of being put in the stocks.

In the Cliveden days only Spike Milligan and the Beatles were really unforgettable. And yet Milligan was as poor as pittance. Throughout the seventies Spike complained whenever we spoke that he could get no work. Was this so? When I questioned his old friend and manager, Norma Farnes, she told me that Spike had been turning down most of the jobs he was offered at the time.

They were both correct. Spike was beginning to make choices. Chiefly he wanted to write; and perform occasionally. Radio and television, he felt, were not really what an artist should be about; too ephemeral. Art must endure.

He wrote six volumes of autobiography: *Adolf Hitler: My Part in His Downfall* (1971); *Rommel? Gunner Who?* (1974); *Monty:*

His Part in My Victory (1976); *Where Have All the Bullets Gone?* (1985) and *Goodbye Soldier* (1986). They show Spike to be a fine historian, and his 'war books' the best satire of armies and war since Jaroslav Hasek wrote *The Good Soldier Schweik*.

The early seventies were a tough time for Milligan: apart from Leo's death, life with Patricia was becoming very strained. Paddie was, in her exactitudes, a bit like Flo. She and Laura were in conflict, partly because of the child's untidiness but really because of her adolescence. It broke Spike's heart when, for the sake of peace, he agreed that Laura should go to school as a weekly boarder, while he resolved to sleep at the office whenever possible.

From as far back as he could remember, Spike had hated the idea of children being separated from their parents. It was something unnatural that in India they associated with the Raj. Certainly Leo would never have allowed his sons to be sent to boarding school. But Paddy would fly into uncontrollable rages and Spike was fearful lest the children be affected by her tirades and his response to them.

Now that the mystery of motherhood was a mystery no longer, sublimating her own career was tougher than Patricia had anticipated. Milligan had suspected as much. Paddy was an enigma. One day we were discussing the Beatles, and Spike said:

> *Their arranger, George Martin, was my best man when I married Paddy. A very nice man. She was very stormy. She had a psychological problem – the father, you know, tried to dominate both his daughters. Like the father of Elizabeth Barrett. The sister went under, but Paddy fought back . . .*

When Spike married her, he said it was as though he and her father had changed places. She wouldn't trust him. She kept her bank account secret. Anything to do with money she would only confer with her brother-in-law. All in all she tried to dominate the children:

> *She did, I'm afraid, dominate Sile. Laura left home, Sean went quiet and he ran away. And then I left home. I didn't want to hurt the children. Children are all that the world is about. I'll never forget that first cup of tea carried on small hands to the door of my bedroom: wobbling it and looking at it very carefully. And then I thought: I'll never get greater moments than this.*

Although he moved out of the house and into his office in the hope that his absence might ease the strain it didn't do any good. He resolved to write himself some hiding-place deep among a forest of words where only characters created by him might enter. He would bury himself in his work. He would forget everything but remembrance – Catford, Bexhill, North Africa and Italy; Bill Hall, Johnny Mulgrew, Norman Vaughan, Harry Secombe, Bernard Montgomery, Toni Pontani and General Rommel.

Edward Heath had come and gone, having played the musical Prime Minister through a winter of discontent with the miners.

In the election of 1974 Wilson retained power with a majority of three, but Spike wasn't in Britain to see that. He was now a sort of globe-trotting guru, mentor to the young, comforter of the disillusioned. He was a much sought-after man.

And then an aberration to end all aberrations. Spike Milligan, socialist and anti-racist, crossed the picket line to perform in South Africa. Here was a man who had been injured, whose friends had been killed fighting the evils of Nazi apartheid in North Africa and Italy, and he had gone off to blackleg on the blacks. Why?

> Even best-sellers take a long time to pay off. I was out of work and broke. And, you know a funny thing? Some of the ground around my house was up for sale. I suddenly realized that I didn't own the bottom of my own garden! Now I would never know if there were fairies there or not.

Milligan thinks that he could change the whole world by slapping a preservation order on it. On the land that he didn't own stood a beautiful weeping ash and near it was a magnificent copper beech tree over a hundred years old. The council put the ground up for sale and told Spike that the trees would have to come down. They wanted twelve thousand pounds and that was exactly the bribe that South Africa dangled in front of the reluctant Milligan. He confused conservation and liberation:

> I hold no brief for South Africa and in my contract I stipulated that I played to black audiences. In fact I outraged my hosts because I insisted on taking the black stage hands with me wherever I went to eat or drink. We went to white restaurants and I was amazed that we were all served. But nobody said a word. I paid the bill and everything was fine.

Milligan's conscience would not allow him to play the apartheid game as required by his South African hosts. He did his best to embarrass white society by keeping company with blacks at all times. He did his one-man show, took his money, and is quite convinced that even if he were willing to go – which he insists he is not – the apartheiders would never again invite him. Did he regret his trip to South Africa?

Bitterly!

But then Spike Milligan really believes in the power of peaceful persuasion. He will keep turning the other cheek long after somebody has cast the first stone:

> *Eccles was really the innocent creature that I was – the one that didn't want to cause any offence and loved simplicity, which I still do. Yes, Eccles was the essential me.*

Milligan is constantly surprised to discover that the world is ill-divided and unfair. In February 1948 he had written that he was now in his thirty-first year and was 'nowhere'. He 'who had never harmed or brought pain to the smallest of God's creatures ... who lives in an attic under three coats loaned by a friend ... and if he never wakens who cares?'

He's not the first writer to have felt like that, and indeed I'd nearly swear that he won't be the last.

Spike is a spokesman for trees and birds, bees, buildings and conservation, for old age, and above all youth. He says he likes to leave law to the lawyers and politics to the politicians. It's not an easy way out; Milligan just feels with his soul.

When *Monty: His Part in My Victory* was first published in 1976, Harold Wilson had resigned and Jim Callaghan had become Prime Minister and leader of the Labour Party. Patricia died of cancer in 1978 and Milligan crucified himself over and over again. Despite all the aggravation, he had loved her, without ever learning the answer to love's bitter mystery.

Twenty-two All for Thespis?

Not bloody likely!

George Bernard Shaw, *Pygmalion*

Spike thought film work wasn't acting at all – too remote. Not that he believed there was anything artificial about appearing before cameras – Spike would be happy with an audience of one. In the beginning he hadn't seen himself as an actor, or any sort of performer:

> *I was terrified, originally. And then, suddenly, one day God said to me, 'Spike, sod it!' – or words to that effect.*

So, he went on the stage and 'didn't give a damn what I did'. He'd come on in a very good suit but very ragged carpet slippers. There was no 'play-on' music – 'in fact they didn't even bother to change the number of the act at the side of the stage'. From the auditorium the audience could hear Milligan squeaking in the wings, 'Boing, boing, boing.'

> *I'd bound onto the stage, 'boing, boing, boing', and say in Eccles' voice, 'Oh, I really must be a terrible disappointment to you all.'*

Two of the films in which he appeared will always be regarded as classics: *The Case of the Mukkinese Battlehorn* and *The Running, Jumping and Standing Still Film*, in which he and Peter Sellers had a hilarious time.

> *I just did everything Dick Lester told me and it worked out fine. Dick is a great film-maker.*

Did he still want to direct?

> *All the time, but they'll never let me. Even after I had directed, very successfully,* The Bed-Sittingroom *for the stage, they wouldn't trust me. There's always that bit missing in my*

television work – the 'Q' series would have been so much better, I always think. But don't start me off on the powers that be at the BBC. I could curse them for a month without ever repeating a swear word.

He loved Sellers. Loved him as a friend and loved working with him. But no way could he have lived in the same house. He had been happy in that room given to him by Peg, and she was very good to him, but Peter? Sellers was an easy man to love but impossible to live with on the same planet:

I think he was permanently dissatisfied with life and if you're dissatisfied with life you wind up banging one of those bloody tambourines in Green Street, singing Hari Krishna because you're totally disillusioned. And in the long run you can't get any more disillusioned than becoming a member of the Hari Krishna sect. It's the ultimate disillusion. And the song is so bad as well, so bloody boring. Of course poor Peter always lacked confidence; a tramp felt more secure than Sellers. Peter lived on the edge, all the time. Did everything on the edge, he even died on the edge. He was what my father would have called 'squanglefied' – all 'squangled' up. The week before he died he rang to tell me that he was very disturbed: 'You know, Spike, I keep changing my will. I've disinherited all my kids because I want to see them make it on their own. . . .'

Spike had admonished Sellers:

'That's a load of crap, Pete. Do you ever stop to think how much easier it might have been for you, if your old man had left you a few bob? Starving in attics gives people pneumonia.'

Peter agreed and said that he would change his will when he got to his solicitors. Sellers died before being able to reinstate his children. After the funeral, Spike told Mrs Sellers of her late husband's intentions. However, being a dutiful widow Lynn Frederick, wishing to respect her husband's intentions, held his last attested will to be sacrosanct.

Of course, after all his heart attacks he was never quite sure about which world he was living in.

I told Milligan that Peter had said he would never again fear death and Spike said it hadn't always been the case:

*He burst into tears at his mother's funeral, and I remember
thinking that it was funny how he went through those same
curtains at Golders Green himself. But I don't know if I'd be
all that gone on cremation. I mean, are the ashes mixed up
with the coffin? To be quite honest, I think I'd like to be buried
– just as long as they wait until I'm dead.*

Death, as a topic for conversation, is a bit like sex – once you
start talking about it you find it difficult to stop. Spike told me:

*I don't really mind – just as long as I'm not around when it
happens. But Peter, after all his heart attacks became a bloody
bore on the subject. It became as if he was always wanting to
die again so as to enjoy the moment and talk about it. Then he
died once too often, didn't he?*

But Milligan hadn't changed his views since he wrote in 1964:

> *Bury me anywhere*
> *Somewhere near a tree*
> *Someplace a horse will graze*
> *And gallop over me*
> *Bury me*
> *Somewhere near a stream*
> *When she floods her banks*
> *I'll give her thanks*
> *For reaching out to me*
> *So bury me – bury me*
> *In my childhood scene*
> *But, please –*
> *Don't burn me*
> *In Golders Green.*[1]

Sellers, to Milligan, was 'Jewish and very round'. Like one
day when he bought Alan Clare, the pianist, an electronic piano,
and then four men came and took it away because he had changed
his mind and given it to Princess Margaret.

Apparently, that was nothing new with Peter. Milligan and he
had a car that they called 'Old Min' after *The Goon Show* character. They originally paid ninety-eight pounds for it and then
Sellers gave Spike a hundred and ten pounds for sole ownership.
Spike then paid Peter two hundred and fifty pounds. Finally
this 'lovely antique' went irrevocably to Sellers for four hundred

pounds. He had it done up at a cost of two thousand pounds and it was in immaculate condition. Milligan says that by now Peter was a very rich man who could afford to indulge his notions:

> Then, one day, he and it arrived at my door and him with a bottle of champagne. 'Look here, Spike,' he said, 'I don't need this car. It really belongs with you because you had it first.' Peter Sellers was chief among 'Indian givers'. When I was in Australia a trailer came and took the car away. I can only guess that it's stowed away in some royal garage these days.

Sellers dearly loved female royalty, but only, as with many well-known mortals, as notches for his conversation. He was a gentle, naïve man of unique thespian talent and not a thought in his head. Milligan told Peter Evans (Sellers' biographer) that Peter was a simpleton, 'the most complex simpleton in the world'. He told me that Sellers had grown up twisted. He thought that Jewish mothers were noted for smothering their would-be messiahs: 'This awful possession of their sons.' I remembered that somebody had said that such a rapport spoiled a boy's future relationships. Milligan told me:

> Peter had quite a few women in tow during his life. Though all the talk about he and Princess Margaret having an affair is a load of nonsense. He would have told me – he always has. I know he made it with that very beautiful Italian actress whose name escapes everybody, that's for sure. And he got very touchy when he thought she was going to make it with me. He needn't have worried – I was in love again then, and besides, her husband never took his eyes off us.

He recalled the incident as his own 'very strange encounter' with the same lady. He and Sellers flew to Rome and, at dinner:

> . . . she put her hand on mine, under the table. And, for a moment, I thought: Is this her Roman way of saying, 'You pay the bloody bill'? Secret sign, you know. I never said anything to Sellers about it because I thought he'd get angry – he was knocking her off at the time. . . . Yes, I liked him very much . . . isn't it very funny that it was me who invited him over (for the last time). 'Do come to Paris with me and Harry and we'll have a drink because we're all getting on.' So he said he'd come. Dear Peter, always very willing. Secombe was much more

*difficult and Bentine more distant . . . and of course he came
over and had this heart attack . . . anything to avoid paying
the bloody bill.*

Hancock was, according to Milligan, 'an insufferable man'.
They got on well together, but 'he was an egomaniac, unbalanced
in the extreme'. He was:

> *neither mean nor generous; right in the middle. . . . He only
> came alive when he was performing and died every time he left
> the stage. . . . He spoke to me two nights before he committed
> suicide. All fun and laughter: 'You really must come out here,
> Spike, it's wonderful.' Hancock was like a snail shell that you
> hoped might have something in it but, when you turned it over,
> it was empty.*

Gradually, Spike noticed, Tony was shedding his partners:
when he left radio he got rid of Kenneth Williams and then
Hattie Jacques. The only one he kept from the old days was Sid
James:

> *I remarked to Galton and Simpson, his writers, 'One day he'll
> get rid of you and then he's going to get rid of himself.' I
> remember very clearly saying that, Ray and Alan were
> standing in my office; and that was precisely what happened.
> Poor Tony, he took himself so seriously, much more seriously
> than any man should.*

Spike admires people who could ad lib. 'Clowns' like Tommy
Cooper who were funny without scripts. Tommy could floor
Milligan by just walking on the stage, without ever doing a thing.
'A clown, you see, the most ancient form of laughter-making,
isn't it?' The other side of that coin was Marty Feldman:

> *He was a droll. I mean if he hadn't had those eyes they would
> never have used him. They used him because of his face. Not
> the first time: Ben Turpin worked because he was cross-eyed.*

He has a lot of time for Barry Humphries and thinks that the
character of Dame Edna Everidge is one of theatre's treasures:

> *He was the first Aussie to take off this awful Australian
> housewife. He is absolutely magnificent. The point about Barry
> is that he's not just a drag artist.*

We talked about female impersonators and I realized just how much he used every canon of living in his work. In his poem 'Unto Us', opposing abortion on demand, he invokes the negative meaning of the showman transvestite to full effect. The unborn child complains:

> . . . There was no Queen's Counsel
> To take my brief.
> The cot I might have warmed
> Stood in Harrod's window.
> When my passing was told
> My father smiled.
> No grief filled my empty space.
> My death was celebrated
> With two tickets to see Danny la Rue
> Who was pretending to be a woman
> Like my mother was.[2]

He believes that actors who invest in the persona of another character, to the extent of dressing as the opposite sex, are very ardent about their profession indeed:

> For the most part [drag artists] take their art very seriously. I'm reading a book called Slapstick and it tells of men who actually walked off the stage because their act was booed. Some actually went and killed themselves.

On the other hand he doesn't think that Bernard Manning 'means anything at all; just an ex-Yiddisha singer who has made a lot of money out of vulgarity'.

Few observers have analysed what makes people laugh more closely than Spike Milligan. Bob Monkhouse is 'a superb professional', but:

> . . . to me he is never funny. What he says is funny – sometimes – but he never is. On the other hand I don't think that other people doing my lines do them the way I see them. Not often. I'm really a one-man show and if I could do all the voices myself I would do them. But, you've got to have actors, you see.

Harry Secombe is funny:

> . . . like a dervish. I'm always waiting for him to break

something. Filled with raspberries and all sorts of double-meaning noises. And of course he's very British. Now that is an impossible thing to be unless, maybe, we're collectively fighting some other country like Germany. Otherwise we are English or Irish or Scots or Welsh. Harry manages to be very pro-British – nearly anti-Welsh. Do you know that he doesn't even go to rugby matches?

And when I was talking about the Plaid Cymru and praising them, Harry came on very strongly against them. But he has this great love of people: when I went to his house-warming party nearly everybody who was anybody was there, but he made straight for me. He has this affection for me.

Milligan thinks that Harry should be as Welsh as Jimmy Edwards was English.

Edwards had a tremendous English ego, you know . . . He came on the stage of the Glasgow Empire just after the interval when the audience had had a good drink, and was bumbling away in this pukka English voice. Some drunk from the Gods shouted, 'Why don't you fuck off back to England!' And he said, 'I will.' Jimmy caught the milk-train home and Joe Loss came up in his place. Poor Joe was so terrified that he put this rumour about that he had lost his trousers so as to be able to appear before the Glaswegians in a kilt.

Twenty years ago Milligan was of the opinion that most things were fair game for the satirist. Now he isn't too sure:

I mean satire should make people laugh and cringe. Now take Mrs Thatcher – and I wish somebody would – but what is there about her that would make any serious person laugh? What she won't do for effect! She was up in Tyneside and the ITN bulletin gave her a very hard time; they said she should have told the people that she was not up to see Middlesborough, but what was left of it. But the BBC just glossed over her visit. It's frightening. The BBC is shit-scared – each man so shit-scared that he will lose his job that most of them will lie, cringe and mope – they will do anything to hold on to their jobs . . .

I wanted to talk about important things, like Sile and Laura expecting his first grandchildren, or how he had kept all his kids' baby words to use in his fairy stories for *The Magic Staircase*, but the 'Iron Lady' was on his mind and he was convinced that she might ensure that no child had any future at all:

> *She has packed the BBC and decreed everything from starvation to war a state secret. It was amazing to see these two newsreels; ITV was so good, so vivid. They made it clear that all Thatcher had gone to see were the things that she had set up there – ignoring the results of what she had set up: unemployment and destitution all over those desolate areas of Tyneside.*

Spike is extremely honest. Whatever dog's chance he had of making his way with the Beeb before now won't be improved if Margaret Hilda knows how he feels about her. I'd like to get him off the question of the PM and onto something pleasant. He's so ingenuous, you see; normally he says the first nice thing that comes into his mouth – unless, of course, he is witnessing injustice:

> *Of course the likes of Mrs Thatcher never listen to anybody. When she was talking to these people in Tyneside, this chap was trying to straighten her out, and she suddenly says, 'No! no! no! no! no!' And she shut him up! She should realize that democracy is all about allowing the people to talk. Thatcher never lets anybody get a word in – she's a marvellous 'word' guardian; she puts up an armoured shield of words against language. She's afraid of communication.*

I honestly wanted to get Spike onto more important matters, so I didn't mention Anthony Sampson and *The Changing Anatomy of Britain*. I wouldn't have got the book finished.

And of course Milligan should talk. A fervent fan of Mrs Thatcher's is the prolific scriptwriter and comic actor, Eric Sykes, and he is a civilization removed from his leader. Eric thought nothing of writing *The Goon Show* for Spike when he was ill. And – now that Milligan brought it up – the two of them have been together since the war. Was there never any conflict? Can a socialist work with a Tory and still make people laugh? Spike beamed and cleared his head of Amazonian ammonites:

> *Yes, Eric is a Tory, but he's so working class it isn't true . . . lives and talks like what he was, a Rochdale mill-worker . . . I suppose he's completely anti-socialist but he's one very dear*

friend who has never let me down . . . forty years . . . a lifetime
. . . Friction? Tories are, in their own eyes, decent enough . . .
it's their outlook that is totally capitalist . . . quite unacceptable
. . . Conflict? It's all very well saying we'll all be rich if we
become Tories, but it can't work out that way – it never has
. . . We've got nearly three million folk out of work and if you
add to that all who are attendant on them, then nearly eight
million people must be affected . . . that's nearly a fifth of the
population! Competition? What's the good of being the fastest
runner in the world if you've got no legs?

About titles? Spike smiled and said to me:

Really, I've been so fortunate . . . one of the other good things
that happened to me because of Bernard Miles and the
Mermaid was getting to know Robert Graves . . . such a
beautiful man . . . such a wonderful writer . . . after a reading
at the Mermaid . . . we sat talking about honours . . . and I
was wondering what people say when they get them . . . Robert
looked up and, smiling, said . . . 'Well, now, Spike, when I got
me OBE I looked Her Majesty straight in the eyes, took her
hand in mine and said, 'Mam, yeh did that very well indeed.'
He was very Irish, you know.

In July 1983, at a Barnet Roman Catholic Church, Spike married Shelagh Sinclair. Sean Milligan was his father's best man
and he remembers that the groom was nervous. The bride remembered that her husband expressed relief that she turned up:
'He said it wouldn't have been much of a wedding on his own.'

Shelagh met him when working as a production assistant for
the BBC. She says she went into his office to find that his whole
life decorated the walls – bits of the past dug out of God knows
where; some of the kids' things from when they were young; an
Irish tricolour draped under a window while Lily Gibbs's trumpet hung over the fire. She remarked on the tricolour and told
him that she was ninety-five per cent Irish. She was Catholic as
well. She says he is the most romantic of suitors. All in all it was
a good basis for a new beginning.

Nowadays, Milligan talks about the work he has on hand. For
Florence Zigfeld Meets McConagle or *The Magic Staircase*, or
countless other projects, there do not seem enough hours in his
day. In Soho in October 1987, one publisher had just newly

published or reissued a 'rake' of Milligan books, and Spike was busier than ever, signing autographs for the populace, and a word to say to everybody or about everybody. Michael Foot sat for a while and Spike told me:

> *A lovely man. Too nice to be a politician. Highly intelligent and everybody knows that you can't be intellectual and head of government. As I wrote in* Puckoon, *'You can fool all the people some of the time but just long enough to be President of the United States.'*

Norma Farnes, who always seems too young to have looked after Milligan and Eric Sykes for so long, kept a genial eye on the many groups, and made sure that, as the celebrations went on and the drink went down, writers were kept as apart as was necessary. Shelagh and I sat and talked and I asked her about some of the poems written to her by Milligan in *Open Heart University* – one or two were hardly about the smooth running of true love. Sweetly she smiled and said:

> *Oh, Dominic, how many people would give how much to have a volume of Spike's verse dedicated to them.*

Milligan, a book on his knee, a pen in his hand, and a queue of friends either wanting his signature or his approval, winked and said mischievously:

> *Her father played for the London Irish, you know – for the rugby team, not the regiment. He was a colonel, so I married up-market.*

I stood with John Antrobus and Roger McGough and we wondered about the Irish obsession – that there would be no death without life without death. We were talking about Joyce and *Ulysses*, but Spike Milligan had his own ideas about it:

> *I've just been reading the Bible where Adam lived to be 930 years. Yeh know, that must have been some bloody insurance premium: imagine being the guy who sold him that policy?*

'The Light that Failed'
To Shelagh

> *It's this darkness at noon –*
> *I can hear the boat sailing*
> *I thought I knew where the switch was*

Everything was so bright,
The picture was nearly finished
Even the eyes seemed perfect
So what happened to the light?
It must have been an eclipse . . .
Mine . . .[3]

Notes

Chapter 1
1. Geoffrey Moorhouse, *India Britannica*, p. 111.
2. James Joyce, *Ulysses*.
3. Cecil Woodham Smith, *The Great Hunger*, p. 20.

Chapter 2
1. Thomas Carlyle, *Heroes and Heroism*.

Chapter 3
1. Quoted by Geoffrey Moorhouse, *India Britannica*, p. 178.
2. Ibid.
3. Ibid.
4. Charles Allen, *The Raj*, p. 105.

Chapter 4
1. Spike Milligan, *Puckoon*.
2. Letter from Leo Milligan to Spike Milligan, 20th April, 1967.

Chapter 5
1. Spike Milligan *The Goon Show Scripts*.
2. R. K. Webb, *Modern England*.
3. Pauline Scudamore, *Spike Milligan – a Biography*, pp. 7–8.
4. Spike Milligan, *Puckoon*.
5. T. P. Kilfeather, *The Connaught Rangers*, p. 131.

Chapter 6
1. Spike Milligan, 'India! India!'.
2. James Joyce, *Portrait of the Artist as a Young Man*.
3. Spike Milligan and John Antrobus, *The Bed-Sittingroom*.
4. Spike Milligan, 'India! India!'
5. Spike Milligan, *The Looney*.
6. Sumit Sarkar, *Modern India*, p. 226.
7. Spike Milligan, 'I Once as a Child', from *Small Dreams of a Scorpion*.

Chapter 7
1. Spike Milligan, 'My Dog Boxer'.
2. Spike Milligan, *The Little Pot Boiler*.

Chapter 8
1. Richard Hoggart, *Speaking to Each Other*, pp. 112–13.

Chapter 9
1. Spike Milligan, 'Indian Boyhood', from *Small Dreams of a Scorpion*.
2. R. K. Webb, *Modern England*, pp. 524–5.

Chapter 10
1. Spike Milligan, letter to *The Times*, 13th June, 1963.
2. Spike Milligan, from *Open Heart University*.
3. Emanuel Shinwell to Dominic Behan.

Chapter 11
1. Spike Milligan, from *Open Heart University*.
2. Lord Byron to Lady Blessington, quoted by Jeffrey Meyers, *Manic Power*.
3. Spike Milligan, from *The Bedside Milligan*.

Chapter 12
1. Spike Milligan, *Adolf Hitler: My Part in His Downfall*.
2. Spike Milligan, article in the *Countryman*, September 1981.

Chapter 13
1. Quoted by Correlli Barnett, *The Audit of War*.
2. Quoted by Richard Hoggart, *Uses of Literacy*.
3. Spike Milligan, 'Small Dreams of a Scorpion'.

Chapter 14
1. Flaubert, translated by Anthony Goldsmith, *L'Education Sentimentale*.
2. Spike Milligan, 'True Love Until', from *Open Heart University*.
3. W. S. Churchill, *The Second World War*, Vol. IV, p. 606.
4. Spike Milligan, 'Longstop Hill', from *The Mirror Running*.
5. Hamish Henderson, *Elegies for the Dead in Cyernaica*.
6. Spike Milligan, *Rommel? Gunner Who?*

Chapter 15
1. Spike Milligan, 'Memory of North Africa', from *The Mirror Running*.
2. Salamander Oasis Trust and Shepherd Walwyn, *Return to Oasis – various war poets*.
3. Spike Milligan, *Monty: His Part in My Victory*.

4. Hamish Henderson, 'D-day Dodgers'.
5. Spike Milligan, 'The Soldiers at Lauro'.
6. Ewan MacColl, 'The Second Front Song'.

Chapter 16
1. Spike Milligan, *Where Have All the Bullets Gone?*
2. Spike Milligan, 'Easter 1916', from *Open Heart University*.
3. Spike Milligan, *Puckoon*.
4. Spike Milligan, 'The Mirror Running' from *The Mirror Running*.
5. Quoted by Pauline Scudamore, *Spike Milligan – a Biography*.
6. Spike Milligan, *Rommel? Gunner Who?*
7. Hamish Henderson, '56th Highland Division's Farewell to Sicily'.

Chapter 17
1. Peter Evans, *Peter Sellers*, p. 57.
2. Ibid., p. 19.
3. Spike Milligan, *Where Have All the Bullets Gone?*
4. Pauline Scudamore, *Spike Milligan – a Biography*, p. 132.

Chapter 18
1. Peter Evans, *Peter Sellers*, p. 65.

Chapter 19
1. Roger Milner, *Reith, The BBC Years*, p. 1.
2. Pauline Scudamore, *Spike Milligan – a Biography*, p. 149.
3. Spike Milligan, *The Goon Show Scripts*.
4. Spike Milligan, *The Mighty Wurlitzer*.
5. Spike Milligan, 'Oberon', from *Small Dreams of a Scorpion*.
6. Pauline Scudamore, *Spike Milligan – a Biography*, p. 174.
7. Ibid., p. 175.

Chapter 20
1. Spike Milligan, *The Mighty Wurlitzer*.
2. André Breton, *Exposition of Surrealism*.
3. Spike Milligan, 'The Sea', from *The Mirror Running*.
4. Bernard Miles, introduction to *The Bed-Sittingroom*.
5. Bernard Miles to Dominic Behan.
6. Spike Milligan and John Antrobus, *The Bed-Sittingroom*.

Chapter 21
1. Letter from Leo Milligan to Spike Milligan, 17th February, 1963.
2. Pauline Scudamore, *Spike Milligan – a Biography*, p. 170.

Chapter 22

1. Spike Milligan, 'Death Wish'.
2. Spike Milligan, 'Unto Us', from *Small Dreams of a Scorpion*.
3. Spike Milligan, 'The Light that Failed'.

Appendix

In all the years Spike Milligan worked for the BBC he was seldom happy and never quite satisfied with their treatment of his work, despite which his shows and those in which he appeared were seldom less than successful and mostly brilliant in conception. I append here a brief résumé of his relationship with the BBC down the years, as written in this biography:

Makes his first television appearance with The Bill Hall Trio, p. 128.
Writes for Jimmy Grafton who is scriptwriter to Derek Roy and *Variety Bandbox*, pp. 133–4.
Writes with Grafton for Alfred Marks, Harry Secombe, Bill Kerr, Dick Emery and Michael Bentine for the BBC, p. 135.
The Goon Show is written for the BBC as *These Crazy People*, p. 135.
Spike likens the BBC to the Kremlin, p. 136.
The BBC make a pilot programme of *The Goon Show*, p. 139.
Denis Main Wilson, the BBC producer, brings Spike, Jimmy Grafton, and Pat Dixon together to script new comedy, p. 139.
After thirteen years *The Goon Show* bows out with *The Last Smoking Seagoon*, p. 141.

Judging by his remarks, time has not softened his attitude to 'BBC bureaucracy'; for example:

He says, on p. 142, that if they employed Van Gogh the BBC would have him painting scenery.
On p. 158, he accuses the BBC of being in the hands of the old-boy network because Huw Wheldon wouldn't allow him to direct.
On p. 164, he suggests that the 'Q' series could have been better had the BBC let him direct it.
On pp. 169–70 he accuses the BBC of bowing to Mrs Thatcher's government.

And yet, it must be said that his successes came most frequently on BBC radio and television.

General Bibliography

Auden, Richard Hoggart (Chatto and Windus, 1951).

Audit of War, The, Correlli Barnett (Macmillan, 1986).

Autobiographies of Sean O'Casey, The (Macmillan, 1963).

Backbench Diaries of Richard Crossman, The, Edited by Janet Morgan (Hamish Hamilton and Jonathan Cape, 1981).

Backward Look, The, Frank O'Connor (Macmillan, 1967).

Balance of Power, A, Jim Prior (Hamish Hamilton, 1986).

British Government and Politics, R. M. Punnett (Heinemann, 1976).

Business in Britain, Graham Turner (Eyre and Spottiswoode, 1969).

Cassino – The Hollow Victory, John Ellis (Andre Deutsch, 1984).

Changing Anatomy of Britain, The, Anthony Sampson (Hodder and Stoughton, 1982).

Chariot of Israel, The, Harold Wilson (Weidenfeld and Nicolson, 1981).

Connaught Rangers, The, T. P. Kilfeather (The Anvil Press).

Defence of the Realm in the 1980s, The, Dan Smith (Croom Helm, 1980).

Eamon de Valera, The Earl of Longford (Hutchinson, 1970).

Elegies for the Dead in Cyernaica, Hamish Henderson (John Lehmann, 1948).

English Economic History, George W. Southgate (J. M. Dent and Sons, 1965).

Freedom at Midnight, Larry Collin/Dominique Lapierre (William Collins, 1975).

Goodbye to All That, Robert Graves (Cassell, 1929).

Gotcha; the Media, the Government and the Falkland Crisis (Faber and Faber).

Governance of Britain, The, Harold Wilson (Weidenfeld and Nicolson and Michael Joseph, 1976).

Great Hunger, The, Cecil Woodham Smith (Hamish Hamilton, 1962).

Harold Wilson – Yorkshire Walter Mitty, Andrew Roth (MacDonald and Jane, 1977).

History of Great Britain, A, R. B. Mowat (Oxford University Press, 1923).

History of Ireland, A, Edmund Curtis (Methuen, 1936).

Identity of Yeats, The, Richard Ellmann (Faber and Faber, 1965).

India Brittanica, Geoffrey Moorhouse (Collins, 1983).

International Gossip, Andrew Borrow (Hamish Hamilton, 1983).

James Joyce, Richard Ellmann (Oxford University Press, 1959).

Making of the English Working Class, The, E. P. Thompson (Pelican, 1968).

Margaret Thatcher, Russell Lewis (Routledge and Kegan Paul, 1975).

Memorials of his Time, Lord Cockburn (T. N. Foulis, 1856).

Memoirs of Richard Nixon (Sidgwick and Jackson, 1978).

Modern England, R. K. Webb (George Allen and Unwin, 1969).

Modern India – 1885–1947, Summit Sarkar (Macmillan, India, 1983).

Nationalisation in British Industry, Leonard Tivey (Jonathan Cape, 1966).

Noël Coward Diaries, The, (Weidenfeld and Nicolson, 1982).

Peter Sellers, the Mask Behind the Mask, Peter Evans (Leslie Frewin, 1969).

Portrait of the Artist as a Young Man, James Joyce (Jonathan Cape, 1948).

Raj, The, Charles Allen (Andre Deutsch, 1975).

Reith, Roger Milner (Mainstream Publishing, 1983).

Second World War, The, Winston Churchill (Cassell, 1951).

Sixties, The, Francis Wheen (Century Publishing, 1982).

Speaking to Each Other, Richard Hoggart (Chatto and Windus, 1971).

Spike Milligan – a Biography, Pauline Scudamore (Granada, 1985).

Stories from the Raj, Selected and Introduced by Saros Cowasjee (Bodley Head, 1982).

Structure and Change in Modern Britain, Trevor Noble (Batsford Academic and Educational Ltd).

Time and Chance, James Callaghan (Collins, 1972).

Ulysses, James Joyce (The Bodley Head, 1960).

Uses of Literacy, Richard Hoggart (Chatto and Windus, 1957).

Milligan in Print

1959   Silly Verses for Kids.
       Values.
1961   A Dustbin of Milligan.
1963   Puckoon.
       The Little Pot Boiler.
1965   A Book of Bits, or a Bit of a Book.
1968   Milliganimals and the Bald-Twit Lion.
1969   The Bedside Milligan.
1970   The Bed-Sittingroom (*with John Antrobus*).
1971   Milligan's Ark.
       Adolf Hitler: My Part in His Downfall.
1972   The Goon Show Scripts.
       Small Dreams of a Scorpion.
1973   Badjelly the Witch.
       The Goon Show Scripts (Second Series).
1974   Rommel? Gunner Who?
       Dip the Puppy.
       Book of the Goons.
       Transports of Delight.
1975   The Great McGonagall Scrapbook.
       The Milligan Book of Records.
1976   Monty: His Part in My Victory.
       William McGonagall: The Truth At Last.
1977   The Spike Milligan Letters (*edited by Norma Farnes*).
1978   Goblins.
       Mussolini: His Part in My Downfall.
1979   Open Heart University.
       The 'Q' Annual.
1980   Get in the 'Q' Annual.
1981   Unspun Socks from a Chicken's Laundry.
       Indefinite Articles and Scunthorpe.
1982   Sir Nobunk and the Dragon.

Goon Show Cartoons.
101 Best and Only Limericks.
1983 There's a Lot of it About.
The Melting Pot.
More Goon Cartoons.
1984 The Spike Milligan Letters Vol. 2
(*edited by Norma Farnes*).
1985 Where Have All the Bullets Gone?
1986 Goodbye Soldier.
1987 The Mirror Running.
Starting Verse for All the Family.
The Looney.

Milligan on TV and Radio

1947 Paging You The Bill Hall Trio (*TV*).
Rooftop Rendezvous The Bill Hall Trio (*TV*).
1949 Opportunity Knocks (*Radio*).
The Bowery Bar (*Radio*).
Hip Hip Hooray (*13 weeks Radio*).
1951 Junior Crazy Gang (The Goon Show, *eleven programmes. Radio.*
Eight series of Goon Shows *in succeeding years*).
Bumblethorpe (*Radio*).
Cinderella (*The Goons appeared as The Goons*).
1952 Goonreel (*TV*).
1953 Milligan in the Frankie Howard Show (*TV*).
1954 Right at the Top (*TV*).
1955 The Lid Off (*TV*).
1956 Idiot Weekly (*TV*).
A Show Called Fred (*TV*).
Son of Fred (*TV*).
Writer of the Year (*TV*).
1963 The Telegoons (*TV*).
Milligan's Wake (*TV*).
Milligan at Large (*TV*).
1965 Muses with Milligan (*TV*).
Q5 (*TV*).
Curry and Chips (*TV*).
1969 The World of Beachcomber (*TV*).
1970 The Other Spike (*Documentary by John Goldschmidt, TV*).

Oh, in Colour (*TV*).

1971   Q6 (*TV*).

1972   The Last Goon Show of All (*TV*).
Marty Feldman's Comedy Machine (*TV*).
A Milligan for all Seasons (*TV*).

1975   The Melting Pot (*TV*).

1977   The Best of British (*TV*).
Q7 (*TV*).
The Best of Fred (*TV*).

1978   Q8 (*TV*).

1980   Q9 (*TV*).

1982   There's a Lot of it About (*TV*).

The foregoing list is incomplete. It would be well nigh impossible to catalogue all Spike Milligan's appearances on Radio and Television. For instance he contributed to this biographer's 'chat show' *Abroad with Behan* (Tyne-Tees TV) and again in 1987 (Radio Telefis Eireann's *Saturday Live*). He has been on *The Wogan Show* (TV) and, as recently as 1988, on *Cover To Cover* (TV). He recently told me that having already been interviewed by Michael Parkinson for *Desert Island Discs* (Radio), Michael invited him back:

Yeh know what happened? Parkinson got the sack!

Milligan on Celluloid

1951   Let's Go Crazy.
Penny Points to Paradise.
London Entertains.

1952   Down among the Z Men.

1953   Super Secret Service.

1956   The Case of the Mukkinese Battlehorn.

1960   The Running, Jumping, and Standing Still Film.
Watch Your Stern.
Suspect.

1961   Invasion Quartet.
What a Whopper.

1962   The Bed-Sittingroom.

1969	The Undertaker.
1970	Magic Christian.
1971	The Magnificent Seven Deadly Sins.
1972	Rentadick.
	Alice's Adventures in Wonderland.
	The Cherry Picker.
1973	Adolf Hitler: My Part in His Downfall.
	Digby, the Biggest Dog in the World.
1974	Man About the House.
	The Great McGonagall.
	The Three Musketeers.
1977	The Last Remake of Beau Geste.
1978	The Hound of the Baskervilles.
1979	The Life of Brian.
1987	Mr H. is Dead.

Milligan on Disc
. . . with the Goons

1956	Bluebottle Blues/I'm Walking Backwards for Christmas. DECCA. F 10756.
	Ying Tong Song/Blodnok's Rock 'n' Roll Call. DECCA. F 10780.
1957	A Russian Love Song/Whistle Your Cares Away. DECCA. 45-F 10945.
	Eeha! Ah! Oh! Ooh!/I Love You. DECCA. 45-F 10885.
1959	Best of the Goon Shows. PARLOPHONE. PMC 1108.
1960	Best of the Goon Shows (2). PARLOPHONE. PMC 1129.
1964	The Goons Unchained Melodies. DECCA. LF 1332.
	How to Win an Election. PHILIPS. AL 3464.
1967	Goon-But not Forgotten. PARLOPHONE. PMC 7037.
1968	Goon Again – Goon Shows. PARLOPHONE. PMC 7062.
1969	World of British Comedy. DECCA. PA 39.
1971	First Men on the Goon. PARLOPHONE. PMC 7132.
1972	The Last Goon Show of All. BBC. REB 142S.
1973	Michael Parkinson Meets the Goons. BBC. REB 165M.
1974	Very Best of the Goons. EMI. EMC 3062.
	Goon Show Classics. BBC. REB 177.
1975	Goon Show Classics. Vol. 2. BBC. REB 213.

1976	Goon Show Classics. Vol. 3. BBC. REB 246.
1977	Goon Show Classics. Vol. 4. BBC. REB 291.
1978	Goon Show Classics. Vol. 5. BBC. REB 339.
1979	Goon Show Classics. Vol. 6. BBC. REB 366.
1980	World of the Goons. DECCA. SPA 569.
	Goon Show Classics. Vol. 7. BBC. REB 392.
1981	Goon Show Classics. Vol. 8. BBC. REB 422.
	Voice Behind the Mask (*Sellers and the Goons. Tribute to Sellers.*) GUILD. 62002A – to D. (Set of 4.)
1982	Goon Show Classics. Vol. 9. BBC. REB 444.

. . . Solo

1956	My September Love/You Gotta Go Oww! PARLOPHONE. R.4251.
1958	Will I find my Love/I wish I knew. PARLOPHONE. R.4406.
1960	Olympic Team/Epilogue. PYE. 7N 15720.
	I'm Walking out with a Mountain/Sewers of the Strand. PARLOPHONE. 45-R 4839.
	Milligan Preserved. PARLOPHONE. (Mono) PMC 1148. (*Stereo*) PCS3018.
1962	Postman's Knock/Wormwood Scrubs Tango. PARLOPHONE. 45-R 4891.
1964	The Best of Milligan's Wake. PYE. NPL 18104.
1965	Muses with Milligan. DECCA. LK4701.
1966	Tower Bridge/Silent Night. PARLOPHONE. R. 5543.
	Purple Aeroplane/Nothing At All. PARLOPHONE. R. 5513.
1968	World of Beachcomber. PYE. NPL 18271.
1969	The Q5 Tune/Ning Nang Nong. PARLOPHONE. R. 5771.
1971	A Record Load of Old Rubbish. BBC. RED 98M.
1974	On the Ning Nang Nong/The Silly Old Baboon. POLYDOR. 2058 524.
	Badjelly the Witch. POLYDOR SELECT. 2460 235.
1980	Puckoon (*excerpts read by Spike*). EMI. SCX 6636.
1981	Adolf Hitler: My Part in His Downfall (*excerpts read by Spike*). COLUMBIA. SCX 6636.
	We are Most Amused. RONCO. RTD 2067A & B (*Double Album for Prince Charles*).
1982	Unspun Socks from a Chicken's Laundry (*Spike reads excerpts from his book of that name*). RIDEDROP SPIKE L1.

Milligan and Company
on disc

1962   Bridge Over the River Wye (*Spike and Others*). PARLO-
        PHONE. Mono: PMC 1190. Stereo: PCS 3018.
1965   Rhymes and Rhythm (*Spike and Others*). ARGO. RG 414-5.
1969   No One's Gonna Change Our World (*Spike and Others*).
        REGAL. SRS 5013.
1972   Alice's Adventures in Wonderland (*Spike and Others*).
        WARNER BROTHERS. K 56009.
1973   World of Children (*Spike and Others*). ARGO. SPA 200.
1974   Cheese/Shipmates (*Spike and Others*). STARLINE. PSR 367.
        He's Innocent of Watergate (*Sellers and Milligan*). DECCA.
        SKL 5194.
        Treasure Island (*Spike and Others*). STARLINE. SRS 5191.
        Live at Cambridge University (*Taylor and Spike*). SPARK.
        SRLO 3001.
1975   Golden Hour of Comedy (*Spike and Others*). GOLDEN
        HOUR. GH 530.
1976   Twenty Golden Giggles (*Spike and Others*). EMI. NTS 125.
        The Snow Goose (*Spike and the London Symphony Orchestra*).
        RCA. RS 1088.
        Forty Years of Television: The Comedians Sing (*Spike and
        Others*). BBC. REB 249.
1979   Sing Songs From Q8 (*Welch and Spike*) UNITED ARTISTES.
        UAG 30223.
        Cavalcade of London Theatre (*Spike and Others*). DECCA.
        D140D-1-4.
1984   Wolves, Witches and Giants (*Welch and Spike*). IMPRESSION
        MIL 2.

Index

Adolf Hitler: My Part in his Downfall, 87–8, 159
Afghanistan, 46–7
Agacote, Maharajah of, 53
Alexander, General, 110
Alexandria, 31
Amalfi, 112, 122
Andrews, Bombadier, 89
Antrim, 1
Antrobus, John, 153, 158, 159, 172
Armstrong, Louis, 103
Askey, Arthur, 142
Associated London Scripts, 159
Associated Press, 71, 72, 90
Astor, Nancy (Lady), 108, 112
Attlee, Clement, 85, 125, 127, 138
Auden, W. H., 135
Australia, 65, 138–9, 147

Baldwin, Stanley, 24, 56, 59
Barry, General Tom, 35
Bart, Lionel, 154
Battle of Britain, 90
BBC, 135, 136, 139, 140–1, 142, 143, 144, 148, 155, 157, 159, 164, 169, 170
Beasley, Tommy, 64
Beatles, the, 159, 160
Bed-Sittingroom, The, 41–2, 153, 158, 163
Behan, Brendan, 122
Bell, Tom, 155
Bentine, Michael, 133, 134, 137, 145, 146, 149, 150, 167
Besant, Annie, 28, 65
Betjeman, John, 136
Bevan, Aneuran, 138
Bexhill-on-Sea, 87, 88, 89, 92, 95, 96, 98, 100, 102, 103
Beyond the Fringe, 155, 158
Bill Hall Trio *see under* Hall, Bill
Blair, Eric *see* Orwell, George
Blackpool: Prince's Theatre, 130
Bombay, 47; Palace Theatre of Varieties, 16

Booth, William, 9–10
Boycott, Captain Charles Cunningham, 10
Brecht, Bertolt, 155
Breton, André, 150–1
Budden, Lt Cecil, 96
Burma, 55, 60

Calcutta, 47
Callaghan, James, 162
Cambridge Footlights, 155
Campaign for Nuclear Disarmament (CND), 147
Carlyle, Thomas, 11, 154
Carson, Edward (Lord), 35
Carter, Kenneth, 113
Case of the Mukkinese Battlehorn, The, 163
Cassino (Monte), 3, 114
Catford, 60, 66, 82, 88
Central Pool of Artistes (CPA), 121, 122, 123, 130
Chamberlain, Neville, 84, 85, 89, 94
Chaplin, Charlie, 12, 157
Charles, Prince of Wales, 4, 140
Churchill, Winston, 32, 46, 56, 59, 85, 97, 98, 104, 106, 120, 125
Clare, Alan, 165
Clark, Major Tony, 117, 120
Cleese, John, 158
Cleverdon, Douglas, 136
Cohen, J. M., 101
Combined Services Entertainments (CSE), 121
Connaught Rangers, 25, 34, 38
Convent of Jesus and Mary, Poona, 43, 56
Cooper, Tommy, 167
Coward, Noël, 125, 155

Daily Herald, 72, 74, 84–5, 127
Daily Mail, 70
Daily Worker, 74
Day, Jumbo, 64
Defoe, Daniel, 45, 46, 52
Delaney, Shelagh, 155

De Valera, Eamon, 46
Diana, Princess of Wales, 4
Dixon, Pat, 139
Donegal, County, 1, 5, 6, 7
Dreaded Batter Pudding Hurler, The, 30–1
Dunkirk, evacuation of, 89
Dunlop, Frank, 153
Dye, Bob (Dipper), 115

Eden, Anthony, 85
Edgington, Harry, 92, 93, 107, 113
Edwards, Jimmy, 169
Eliot, T. S., 136
Emery, Dick, 135
Enniskillens, 25, 38
ENSA, 16, 103
Eton, Peter, 148
Evans, Peter, 129, 166

Fallon, Jack, 80, 81
Farnes, Norma, 159, 172
Feldman, Marty, 167
Finney, Albert, 155
Flaubert, Gustave, 93, 100, 101
Florence Zigfeld Meets McConagle, 171
Foot, Michael, 147, 172
Franco, General, 73
Frank Weir Orchestra, 137
Frederick, Lynn, 164
Fry, Christopher, 136

Gaitskell, Hugh, 138
Gallagher, Willie, 128
Galton, Ray, 159, 167
Gandhi, Mahatma, 29, 47, 65
Gann, Leo *see under* Gorden, Gwen
Garnett, Alf, 155
Gauguin, Paul, 119
George V, King, 38
George VI, King, 85
Getty, Paul, 4
Gibbs, Lily, 82, 84, 85, 90–1, 100, 101, 123, 124, 130, 132
Gilliam, Lawrence, 135, 136
Gilliam, Terry, 158
Glasgow: Empire, 169; Pavilion, 130; Theatre Royal, 13
Goldsmith, Lt Anthony, 93, 95, 96, 100, 101, 106, 107, 109, 118, 154
Goldsmith's College, 79, 137, 138
Goncharov, Ivan Aleksandrovich, 153
Goodbye Soldier, 123, 127, 160
Goon Show, The, 33, 52, 74, 75, 79, 136, 139, 140, 141, 142, 143–4, 148, 149, 150, 165, 170
Goons, the, 22, 134, 143–4, 150, 155, 158
Gorden, Gwen and Gann, Leo, 13, 16, 28, 68, 69
Grafton Arms, 138

Grafton, Jimmy, 133, 134, 135, 136, 139
Graves, Robert, 135, 136, 159, 171
Greene, Graham, 83
Grierson, John, 135

Haig, General Douglas, 127
Haines, Arthur, 142
Hall, Bill, 123, 126, 127, 128, 131, 154, 161; and Bill Hall Trio, 80, 123, 127, 128, 129, 130, 158
Hall, Nina, 76–7
Hancock, Tony, 142, 167
Harlem Club Band, 81
Heath, Edward, 161
Hemingway, Ernest, 15
Henderson, Hamish, 106, 108, 112
Higgins, Elizabeth (Mrs William Patrick Milligan), 10
Hill, Benny, 113, 133
Hitler, Adolf, 84, 97, 98, 105
Hoggart, Richard, 59, 96, 102
Hopkins, Gerard Manley, 101
Humphries, Barry, 167

India, 1, 13, 14, 16–19, 46, 47, 50, 56, 100
'India! India!', 43
'Indian Boyhood', 64
Ireland and the Irish, 1, 2, 3, 4, 5, 8, 11, 23, 28, 34–5, 38 *et passim*; and 1916 Easter Rising, 23, 25, 34, 117, 118
Italian Communist Party, 131

James, Sid, 167
Jenkins, Jumbo, 103
Johnson, Dr Samuel, 24, 31
Jones, Terry, 158
Joyce, James, 2, 21, 52, 58, 101, 151, 172; *Ulysses*, 2, 58

Kavanagh, Henry, 2
Kennedy, Elizabeth Louise (Mrs Michael Patrick Milligan; maternal great-grand-mother), 5, 6, 9
Kennedy, Jacqueline, 6–7
Kennedy, President John F. and family, 2, 6
Kerr, Bill, 135
Kettleband, Alfred H. (maternal grand-father), 1, 7, 14, 28, 35, 39, 42–3, 52, 55, 62
Kettleband, Mrs A. H., née Ryan (mater-nal grandmother), 7, 8, 42, 55, 57, 128
Kettleband, Eileen (aunt), 28, 30, 42, 62, 63
Kettleband, Flo *see* Milligan, Flo
Kettleband, Hughie (uncle), 42, 43, 57, 68

Laski, Marghanita, 149
Lauro, 113, 114, 115, 117

Lenihan, Marie, 33
Lennon, John, 159
Leno, Dan, 146
Lester, Dick, 163
Lewis, Wyndham, 2
Little Pot Boiler, The, 52
Littlewood, Joan, 155
Lloyd George, David, 29, 46
Looney, The, 25, 45, 154
Loss, Joe, 139, 169
Lucknow, siege of, 1, 2
Lyric, Hammersmith, 153, 154

MacDonald, Ramsay, 55, 59, 63, 72, 73
McGough, Roger, 172
McIntyre, Brian, 62, 63
MacLiammoir, Michael, 158
Macmillan, Harold, 154, 159
MacNeice, Louis, 135, 136, 141
MacReady, General Nevil, 46
Maddaloni Barracks, 119, 120
Magic Staircase, The, 169, 171
manic depression, 79–80, 120, 145, 157
Manning, Bernard, 168
Margaret, Princess, 165, 166
Marks, Alfred, 135
Marlowe, June (first Mrs Spike Milligan), 140, 144, 148
Martin, George, 160
Memory of North Africa, 109
Men in Gitis, 121, 125, 131
Mermaid Theatre, 152, 171
Meyers, Jeffrey, 79
Mighty Wurlitzer, The, 150
Miles, Bernard, 152–3, 171
Milligan, Desmond (brother), 9, 56, 58, 59, 60, 62, 65, 66, 68, 70, 81, 83, 94, 125, 126, 128, 137, 138, 139, 147, 155
Milligan, Elizabeth Louise *see* Kennedy, Elizabeth Louise
Milligan, Flo (née Kettleband, Margaret Flora; mother), 1, 4, 7, 9, 13, 14, 24–5, 28, 29, 30, 32, 33, 39, 40, 42, 43, 44, 53, 54, 55–6, 59, 61, 62, 63, 65–6, 67, 68–9, 75, 78, 81, 82, 83, 85–6, 87, 94, 98, 102, 126–7, 128, 129, 137, 138, 147, 149, 155, 156, 157
Milligan, Jane (daughter), 155
Milligan, June *see* Marlowe, June
Milligan, Kathleen (Mrs Alf Thurgar; aunt), 10, 32, 44, 70, 83
Milligan, Laura (daughter), 3, 144, 152, 160
Milligan, Leo Alphonso (father), 1, 3, 4, 6, 7, 11–12, 13; marriage, 14, 24–5; and First World War, 20–2, 28; in India, 16–19, 24, 28, 29, 30, 31–2, 33, 34–5, 36, 37, 39, 40–1, 42–5, 46, 47, 49–50, 53–4, 111, 113; in Burma, 55, 56, 57, 58, 59,

60, 62, 63; on leaving army for England, 63, 65–6; in England, 67, 68–9, 70–1, 72, 74, 75, 77, 78, 81, 84, 85, 86, 90, 125, 126, 127, 128, 137; and emigration to Australia, 138–9; death, 155, 156; character, 157
Milligan, Michael Patrick (great-grandfather), 1, 5, 6, 7, 13
Milligan, Patricia *see* Ridgeway, Patricia
Milligan, Sean (son), 3, 147, 152, 160, 171
Milligan, Shelagh *see* Sinclair, Shelagh
Milligan, Sile (daughter), 3, 47, 152, 160
Milligan, Spike (Terence Alan): family background, 1–8, 9–14, 16–22, 24; birth, 29; childhood in India, 30, 31, 32–3, 34, 35, 39–40, 42–7, 48–54, 61; and in Burma, 55, 56–9, 61–5; on family home leave in 1931, 59–60, 61; leaves India, 65, 66; youth in Catford, 66–7, 68–70, 71, 73–4, 75–7; as member of band, 74, 78–9, 80–1; and Second World War, 15–16, 22, 87–93, 94–9, 100–7, 108–16, 117–24; and return from war, 125–7; with Bill Hall Trio, 128–32; meets Jimmy Grafton, 133–5; as comedy writer, 135–7, 139–40; and *The Goon Show*, 140–4, 145, 149–51; marriage to June Marlowe, 140, 144, 147; and later artistic career, 151–5, 157–63; marriage to Patricia Ridgeway, 154, 160–1, 162; death of father, 156–7; marriage to Shelagh Sinclair, 171; and relationship with father, 21–2, 46, 137–8, 156–7; and with mother, 33–4, 39, 42, 82, 85–6, 94, 126–7; on Ireland and Irishness, 23–4, 27–8, 35, 36, 37; on Catholicism and Christianity, 40, 41–2, 52–3, 69, 83; and manic depression, 79–80, 120, 145, 157
Milligan, William Patrick (grandfather), 6, 7, 9, 10–11, 12, 13, 20, 25, 26, 34, 35, 37, 44, 59
Milligan, William Patrick Marmaduke (uncle), 11, 54
Milner, Roger, 141
'Monkenhurst', 31
Monkhouse, Bob, 168
Montgomery, General, 98, 161
Monty: His Part in My Victory, 159–60, 162
Monty Python, 155, 158
Mosley, Sir Oswald, 70, 73
Mulgrew, Johnny, 127, 128, 131, 161
Munnings, Hilda *see* Sokolova, Lydia
Murdoch, Richard, 142
Muses with Milligan, 157–8
Mussolini, Benito, 98

Nathan, David, 158
Naughton, Bill, 88

Nehru, Pandit, 53–65
New Era Rhythym Boys, 74
Norman, Frank, 154
Nuffield Centre, 136

Oblomov, 153–4; see also Son of Oblomov
O'Connor, General Richard, 110
Open Heart University, 71–2, 172
O'Raghailly, Tomas, 25
Orwell, George, 58–9
O'Toole, Peter, 155
Over the Page, 121, 122, 123

Palin, Michael, 158
Parnell, Val, 128
Pearse, P. H., 117, 118
Peltier, René, 135–6
Pinter, Harold, 155
Piratin, Phil, 127
Pontani, Antoinette (Toni), 123, 124, 126, 130, 131, 132, 161
Poona, 14, 24, 28, 34, 39, 41, 53, 54, 56, 57, 62, 65, 100, 137
Poplar, London, 69; Queen's Palace of Varieties, 12, 13
Portici Officers' Club, 119
Puckoon, 25, 26–7, 34, 35, 36–7, 52, 79, 117, 118, 154, 172

'Q' series, 155, 158, 164

Raj, the, 17–20, 43, 44, 50, 56, 65, 102
Rangoon, 56, 57, 60, 61, 64, 137
Rattigan, Terence, 93
Reith, John (Lord), 141
Return to Oasis, 110
Ridgeway, Patricia ('Paddy'; second Mrs Spike Milligan), 3, 154, 160–1, 162
Robb, Lieutenant, 120, 121
Roberts, Kathleen (Mrs Desmond Milligan), 128, 138
Robinson Crusoe, 31, 45, 46, 52, 53, 95, 157
Robson, Joe, 147–8
Rocca family, 132
Rommel, General Irwin, 98, 110, 161
Rommel? Gunner Who?, 107, 122, 159
Roosevelt, President Franklyn D., 104
Rothermere, Lord, 70, 73
Routh, Sir Randolph, 8
Roy, Derek, 133, 135
Royal Artillery, 9, 21, 25, 38, 99, 109
Rudden, Father, 29, 35, 36
Running, Jumping and Standing Still Film, The, 163
Russell, Bertrand, 128, 147, 159

St Paul's Roman Catholic School, Rangoon, 57
Salerno, 22, 111

Scudamore, Pauline, 48, 141
Secombe, Harry, 32, 57, 113, 121, 122, 123, 130, 133, 134, 135, 136, 137, 145, 146, 149, 150, 161, 166, 168–9
Sellers, Peg, 129, 139, 164
Sellers, Peter, 23, 57, 122, 129, 130, 133, 134, 137, 145, 146–7, 149, 150, 163, 164–7
Shaw, George Bernard, 8
Shinwell, Emanuel, 72–3, 127–8
Sillitoe, Alan, 154
Silly Verses for Kids, 152, 154
Simpson, Alan, 159, 167
Simpson, Wallis, 81
Sinclair, Shelagh (third Mrs Spike Milligan), 171, 172
Singer, James Burns, 135
Sligo, County, 7, 8, 9
Sokolova, Lydia, 13
'Soldiers at Lauro', 114
Son of Oblomov, 154
South Africa, 161–2
Speight, Johnny, 142, 159
Stephens, Larry, 144
Stokes, Major, 88, 93
Stones of Deptford, 71
Swift, Jonathan, 22, 23, 30, 147
Swiss Family Robinson, 45, 46, 95
Sykes, Eric, 144, 145, 159, 170–1, 172
Synge, J. M., 152

Telegoons, The, 158
Thatcher, Margaret, 141, 169, 170
That Was The Week That Was, 155
Thomas, Dylan, 135, 136, 141, 142–3; Under Milkwood, 135, 142
Thompson, David, 141
Those Crazy People, 139, 140
Thurber, James, 79
Thurgar, Alf, 83
Thurgar, Kathleen see Milligan, Kathleen
Thurgar, Terry, 83
Toulouse-Lautrec, Henri, 52, 119
Townshend, General, 21, 28
Treasure Island, 153
Tripoli, 106
Tunis, 107, 110, 111

Ustinov, Peter, 158

Valjean Times, 121
Van Dams, 131
Van Gogh, Vincent, 37, 119, 142
Variety Bandbox, 133
Vaughan, Norman, 123, 130, 131, 161
Victoria, Queen, 5
Vidal, Gore, 112

Waugh, Evelyn, 83

Webb, R. K., 32, 98
Wheldon, Huw, 157, 158
Where Have All the Bullets Gone?, 117, 130, 136, 160
Wilde, Oscar, 84, 155
Wilkins, Dave, 24
Williams, Kenneth, 167
Wilson, Denis Main, 139
Wilson, Harold, 138, 155, 161, 162

Windmill Theatre, London, 130
Windsor, Duke of, 84
Winters, Mike and Bernie, 63
Wood, Brigadier, 121, 123
Woolwich Arsenal, 9, 73, 74, 81
Woolwich Garrison Theatre, 13
Wyss, Jan, 45, 46, 52

Yeats, W. B., 6, 27, 112, 118

A Selected List of Non-Fiction Available from Mandarin Books

While every effort is made to keep prices low, it is sometimes necessary to increase prices at short notice. Mandarin Paperbacks reserves the right to show new retail prices on covers which may differ from those previously advertised in the text or elsewhere.

The prices shown below were correct at the time of going to press.

☐	7493 0000 0	**Moonwalk**	Michael Jackson	£3.99
☐	7493 0004 3	**South Africa**	Graham Leach	£3.99
☐	7493 0010 8	**What Fresh Hell is This?**	Marion Meade	£3.99
☐	7493 0011 6	**War Games**	Thomas Allen	£3.99
☐	7493 0013 2	**The Crash**	Mihir Bose	£4.99
☐	7493 0014 0	**The Demon Drink**	Jancis Robinson	£4.99
☐	7493 0015 9	**The Health Scandal**	Vernon Coleman	£4.99
☐	7493 0016 7	**Vietnam – The 10,000 Day War**	Michael Maclear	£3.99
☐	7493 0049 3	**The Spycatcher Trial**	Malcolm Turnbull	£3.99
☐	7493 0022 1	**The Super Saleswoman**	Janet Macdonald	£4.99
☐	7493 0023 X	**What's Wrong With Your Rights?**	Cook/Tate	£4.99
☐	7493 0024 8	**Mary and Richard**	Michael Burn	£3.50
☐	7493 0061 2	**Voyager**	Yeager/Rutan	£3.99
☐	7493 0060 4	**The Fashion Conspiracy**	Nicholas Coleridge	£3.99
☐	7493 0027 2	**Journey Without End**	David Bolton	£3.99
☐	7493 0028 0	**The Common Thread**	Common Thread	£4.99

All these books are available at your bookshop or newsagent, or can be ordered direct from the publisher. Just tick the titles you want and fill in the form below.

Mandarin Paperbacks, Cash Sales Department, PO Box 11, Falmouth, Cornwall TR10 9EN.

Please send cheque or postal order, no currency, for purchase price quoted and allow the following for postage and packing:

UK	55p for the first book, 22p for the second book and 14p for each additional book ordered to a maximum charge of £1.75.
BFPO and Eire	55p for the first book, 22p for the second book and 14p for each of the next seven books, thereafter 8p per book.
Overseas Customers	£1.00 for the first book plus 25p per copy for each additional book.

NAME (Block Letters) ....

ADDRESS ....

....